Presented to:

_____

By:

_____

GRACE

for the Moment®

FAMILY DEVOTIONAL

100 Devotions for Families to Enjoy God's Grace

MAX LUCADO

THOMAS NELSON
Since 1798

Dear Families,

Just like parents take care of their children and provide for them, God provides for and takes care of his children. He gives us what we need: hope and forgiveness and joy. He comforts our sadness. And, most important, he gives us grace.

Grace is God saying, "I know you've messed up, but I still love you anyway." Grace is when you tell God you're sorry and he says, "You're forgiven." One of my favorite Bible verses explains it like this: "Let us, then, feel free to come before God's throne. Here there is grace. And we can receive mercy and grace to help us when we need it" (Hebrews 4:16).

You can't always choose what happens in your day. But you can choose how you think about it and what you do about it. You can choose to worship God as a family. Each entry in *Grace for the Moment® Family Devotional* includes an adult devotion from *Grace for the Moment®* and a corresponding children's devotion from *Grace for the Moment®: 365 Devotions for Kids*. Parents and children can read their devotions separately or together and then come together to read the key verse aloud to dig deeper into the day's entries. The "Grow in Grace" sections are thoughts and questions designed to draw you closer to the God of grace as you spend time together.

MAX LUCADO

A Chosen People

Do you ever feel unnoticed? New clothes and styles may help for a while. But if you want permanent change, learn to see yourself as God sees you: "He has covered me with clothes of salvation and wrapped me with a coat of goodness, like a bridegroom dressed for his wedding, like a bride dressed in jewels" (Isaiah 61:10).

Does your self-esteem ever sag? When it does, remember what you are worth. "You were bought, not with something that ruins like gold or silver, but with the precious blood of Christ, who was like a pure and perfect lamb" (1 Peter 1:18–19).

The challenge is to remember that. To meditate on it. To focus on it. To allow his love to change the way you look at you.

When Christ Comes

Read Together

You are a chosen people, royal priests, a holy nation, a people for God's own possession.

I PETER 2:9

2

God Chooses You

Do you ever feel invisible? As if nobody even notices you? *Maybe some new clothes will get me noticed,* you think. And maybe they do. For a little while. But then the latest craze is yesterday's news, and you're back to . . . invisible. Want a change that lasts? Learn to see yourself as God sees you—covered with the "clothes of salvation" and wrapped in "a coat of goodness" (Isaiah 61:10 ICB).

Do you ever feel like a nobody? When you do, remember what you are really worth. Remember what—or rather who—God gave to save you: "You were bought with the precious blood of the death of Christ, who was like a pure and perfect lamb" (1 Peter 1:19).

If you ever start to feel invisible or left out, remember this: God *chooses* you to be his child. That can be hard to remember sometimes. So pray about it. Think about it. Let the way God sees you change the way you see yourself.

GROWING IN GRACE

God chooses to see you as his wonderful creation. How do you choose to see your family and friends? They are each a wonderful creation of God. Your mom. Your dad. Even your sister and brother. Find something you love about each of your family members and friends—then tell them what it is.

3

A Complete Restoration

God loves to decorate. God *has* to decorate. Let him live long enough in a heart, and that heart will begin to change. Portraits of hurt will be replaced by landscapes of grace. Walls of anger will be demolished and shaky foundations restored. God can no more leave a life unchanged than a mother can leave her child's tear untouched . . . . .

This might explain some of the discomfort in your life. Remodeling of the heart is not always pleasant. We don't object when the Carpenter adds a few shelves, but he's been known to gut the entire west wing. He has such high aspirations for you. God envisions a complete restoration. He won't stop until he is finished . . . . He wants you to be just like Jesus.

Just Like Jesus

Read Together

You will know that God's power is very great for us who believe.

EPHESIANS 1:19

You know the Father. . . . The word of God lives in you.

1 JOHN 2:14 ICB

God Lives Here

Have you ever done any decorating in your room? Maybe you added a poster here. Put out a favorite collection there. Maybe you even got to pick the color for the walls. You added this and changed that until it looked like *you* lived there.

Well, God loves to decorate too. Actually, God *has* to decorate. Let him live long enough in a heart, and that heart will begin to change. He'll move some forgiveness into that corner. He'll add some shelves and fill them up with his Word. It's not always pleasant though. You might feel a little uncomfortable when he knocks down that wall of jealousy or anger, but that new spirit of kindness he puts in will look and feel great. Then he'll paint your whole heart with love—love for him and love for others.

God wants to give your heart a complete makeover. So he won't stop working until he's completely finished—until it looks just like *he* lives there.

GROWING IN GRACE

Decorate your room with God's Word. Write favorite Bible verses on sticky notes. Then stick them by your light switch, above your pillow, or anywhere else you're sure to see them. God loves it when you make "room" for him!

The Foundation of Courage

"Therefore, there is now no condemnation for those who are in Christ Jesus" (Romans 8:1 NIV).

"[God] justifies those who have faith in Jesus" (Romans 3:26 NIV).

For those in Christ, these promises are not only a source of joy. They are also the foundations of true courage. You are guaranteed that your sins will be filtered through, hidden in, and screened out by the sacrifice of Jesus. When God looks at you, he doesn't see you; he sees the One who surrounds you. That means that failure is not a concern for you. Your victory is secure. How could you not be courageous?

The Applause of Heaven

Read Together

"I will forgive their wickedness and will remember their sins no more."

HEBREWS 8:12 NIV

Be Brave!

The Bible says that "those who are in Christ Jesus are not judged guilty" (Romans 8:1 ICB). It also says that God will "make right any person who has faith in Jesus" (3:26 ICB).

That is great news for God's children! Because sometimes, even when you *want* to do right, you do wrong. We all do. That's why God's promises are so wonderful! If you believe in Jesus and obey him, God promises that your sins will all be taken away and that they will be hidden by Jesus. So when God looks at you, he doesn't see your sin; he sees the One who saves you—Jesus.

That means that you don't have to worry about messing up. You've already won because Jesus saves you. Trusting in that promise gives you the courage to try to do the right thing—even when you know you might mess up. Trusting in that promise lets you be brave.

GROWING IN GRACE

Grab some friends and play a game of hide-and-seek. As you hide, remember how Jesus hides your sins and mistakes. And as you seek, remember how God promises never to seek for your forgiven sins!

Our High Priest

Read how J. B. Phillips translates Hebrews 4:15:

For we have no superhuman High Priest to whom our weaknesses are unintelligible—he himself has shared fully in all our experience of temptation, except that he never sinned.

It's as if he knows that we will say to God: "God, it's easy for you up there. You don't know how hard it is from down here." So he boldly proclaims Jesus' ability to understand. Look at the wording again.

He himself. Not an angel. Not an ambassador. Not an emissary, but Jesus himself.

Shared fully. Not partially. Not nearly. Not to a large degree. Entirely! Jesus shared fully.

In all our experience. Every hurt. Each ache. All the stresses and all the strains. No exceptions. No substitutes. Why? So he could sympathize with our weaknesses.

In the Eye of the Storm

Read Together

Our high priest is able to understand our weaknesses. He was tempted in every way that we are, but he did not sin.

HEBREWS 4:15

8

Jesus Knows

Some people might think, *Jesus, it's easy for you up there. You're in heaven. You just don't know how hard it is down here.* But those people would be wrong. The Bible says he "is able to understand" (Hebrews 4:15 ICB).

Jesus knows. He knows because he *himself* left heaven and came to earth. He didn't send an angel or a messenger. And he didn't come as God. He made himself completely human.

Do you ever feel angry, scared, or left out? Jesus did. Did you know that Jesus was once your age? He had parents to obey and brothers and sisters to get along with. He fell down, and he fell asleep. He went to school and played with friends. He was laughed at, and he was hurt.

Jesus knows everything you're going through. It's one of the reasons he came to earth—so he would know what it feels like. And so he could help you get through it.

GROWING IN GRACE

Jesus can help you because he's "been there and done that." Is there someone you can help because you've been there and done that? Teach a younger child to catch a ball. Walk with a frightened preschooler to Bible class. Help your brother or sister study for a test.

Who Is the Servant?

Martha is worried about something good. She's having Jesus over for dinner. She's literally serving God. Her aim was to please Jesus. But she made a common, yet dangerous mistake. As she began to work for him, her work became more important than her Lord. What began as a way to serve Jesus, slowly and subtly became a way to serve self. . . . She has forgotten that the meal is to honor Jesus, not Martha. . . .

It's easy to forget who is the servant and who is to be served.

He Still Moves Stones

Read Together

Martha was distracted with much serving . . . . "But . . . Mary has chosen that good part, which will not be taken away from her."

LUKE 10:40–42 NKJV

Serving Jesus

Martha was a dear friend of Jesus. But the Bible tells us about a time when she was worried. She was having Jesus over for dinner. She was *really* going to be serving God! She wanted everything to be just right for Jesus. But she made one very big mistake. She was working so hard for Jesus that she let her work become more important than her Lord.

You see, Martha wanted Jesus to praise *her* for all her work. She forgot that she was supposed to be praising *him* with her work. She forgot that the meal was to honor Jesus. What began as a way to serve Jesus turned into a way to serve herself.

It is important to serve Jesus. But don't serve him just so that others will see you. Don't serve him so that others will be pleased with you or say nice things about you. Remember—you are the servant, and he is the One to be served.

GROWING IN GRACE

Want to make sure you are serving Jesus and not yourself? Serve in secret. Find something you can do—take out the trash, feed the dog, water the plants—but don't let anyone know you did it. Secret servants make God smile.

Sowing Seeds of Peace

Want to see a miracle? Plant a word of love heart-deep in a person's life. Nurture it with a smile and a prayer, and watch what happens.

An employee gets a compliment. A wife receives a bouquet of flowers. A cake is baked and carried next door. A widow is hugged. A gas-station attendant is honored. A preacher is praised.

Sowing seeds of peace is like sowing beans. You don't know why it works; you just know it does. Seeds are planted, and topsoils of hurt are shoved away.

Don't forget the principle. Never underestimate the power of a seed.

The Applause of Heaven

Read Together

"Plant goodness, harvest the fruit of loyalty, plow the new ground of knowledge."

HOSEA 10:12

Planting Seeds of Kindness

Want to see a miracle? Plant a kind word in the heart of someone who is sad and hurting. Water it with a prayer and add a sunny smile—and then watch what happens.

Want to see some more miracles? Fix a snack for your mom or dad without being asked. Smile at your teacher just because. Give a friend a pat on the back when she's had a tough day. Draw something special for a person who is sick. Bring in the mail or the newspaper for an older neighbor. Offer to clean up even when it's not your turn.

Sowing seeds of kindness is like sowing beans. You don't know how they grow or why; you just know they do. And somehow that one little seed of kindness that you plant will grow into a whole garden of good deeds.

Never doubt the power of a seed.

GROWING IN GRACE

Sow some flower seeds. Fill each cup of an egg carton with dirt. Poke a seed—like petunias or snapdragons—into each cup. Add a little water and sunshine. As they grow, think about how they started from tiny seeds. What do you think will grow from a seed of kindness?

You're Something Special

We want to know how long God's love will endure . . . . Not just on Easter Sunday when our shoes are shined and our hair is fixed. . . . Not when I'm peppy and positive and ready to tackle world hunger. Not then. I know how he feels about me then. Even I like me then.

I want to know how he feels about me when I snap at anything that moves, when my thoughts are gutter-level, when my tongue is sharp enough to slice a rock. How does he feel about me then? . . .

Can anything separate us from the love Christ has for us?

God answered our question before we asked it. So we'd see his answer, he lit the sky with a star. So we'd hear it, he filled the night with a choir; and so we'd believe it, he did what no man had ever dreamed. He became flesh and dwelt among us.

He placed his hand on the shoulder of humanity and said, "You're something special."

In the Grip of Grace

Read Together

Nothing . . . in the whole world will ever be able to separate us from the love of God.

Romans 8:39

You're Something Special

How long will God love you?

Not just on Easter Sunday when your shoes are shined and your hair is fixed. Not just when you're happy and kind. Not just then. Everybody loves you then.

But how will God feel about you when you snap at everyone around you? When you have hateful thoughts? When you sass your parents? How does God feel about you then?

Can anything separate you from the love Jesus has for you?

God answered that question long before you even asked it. He answered it by lighting up the sky with a star. He answered it by waking the shepherds with the song of angels. He answered it by sending his one and only Son to be born in a stable in Bethlehem—to save you.

By sending Jesus to live and die on earth, God said to all people, "You're something special. Nothing can keep me from loving you."

GROWING IN GRACE

Bad days happen. They just do. Next time you're feeling rotten—or when you've been rotten—ask your mom if you can use a dry erase marker on the mirror. Look at yourself in the mirror and draw a big heart around your face. Then write "Jesus loves me—even today."

God Heals Our Hurts

The Greek word for compassion is *splanchnizomai,* which won't mean much to you unless you are in the health professions and studied "splanchnology" in school. If so, you remember that "splanchnology" is a study of . . . the gut.

When Matthew writes that Jesus had compassion on the people, he is not saying that Jesus felt casual pity for them. No, the term is far more graphic. Matthew is saying that Jesus felt their hurt in his gut:

He felt the limp of the crippled.

He felt the hurt of the diseased.

He felt the loneliness of the leper.

He felt the embarrassment of the sinful.

And once he felt their hurts, he couldn't help but heal their hurts.

In the Eye of the Storm

Read Together

He had compassion on them.

MATTHEW 14:14 NIV

Jesus Feels Our Hurts

The book of Matthew was first written in Greek. The Greek word for "felt sorry" is *splanchnizomai*. Since you probably haven't studied *splanchnizomai* in school, this word won't mean much to you. But what it means is "in the gut."

So when Matthew wrote that Jesus felt sorry for the people, he didn't mean that Jesus just felt a little sad for them. No, it is far more powerful. Matthew was saying that Jesus felt their hurt like a punch in the gut:

He felt the limp of the crippled.
He felt the hurt of the sick.
He felt the loneliness of the leper.
He felt the shame of the sinful.

And once Jesus felt their hurts, he couldn't help but heal their hurts.

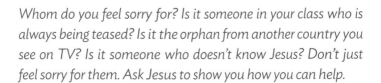

GROWING IN GRACE

Whom do you feel sorry for? Is it someone in your class who is always being teased? Is it the orphan from another country you see on TV? Is it someone who doesn't know Jesus? Don't just feel sorry for them. Ask Jesus to show you how you can help.

Your Day Is Coming

Some of you have never won a prize in your life. Oh, maybe you were quartermaster in your Boy Scout troop or in charge of sodas at the homeroom Christmas party, but that's about it. You've never won much. You've watched the Mark McGwires of this world carry home the trophies and walk away with the ribbons. All you have are "almosts" and "what-ifs."

If that hits home, then you'll cherish this promise: "And when the Chief Shepherd appears, you will receive the crown of glory that will never fade away" (1 Peter 5:4 NIV).

Your day is coming. What the world has overlooked, your Father has remembered, and sooner than you can imagine, you will be blessed by him.

When Christ Comes

Read Together

"Hold on to what you have, so that no one will take your crown."

REVELATION 3:11 NIV

Your Turn Is Coming

Some of you have never won a prize in your life. Oh, maybe you got a ribbon at field day for participation. Maybe you even won a cheap toy at the balloon-pop game at the fair. But you've never won anything really big. You've watched the stars of this world carry home the trophies and the blue ribbons. All you have are "almosts" and "could-have-beens."

If that sounds like you, then you'll love this promise: "When Christ, the Head Shepherd, comes, you will get a crown. This crown will be glorious, and it will never lose its beauty" (1 Peter 5:4 ICB).

Your turn is coming! The world may not see how great you are, but your Father does. And sooner than you can imagine, you will be blessed by him!

GROWING IN GRACE

Make your own crown from poster board. Cut a piece long enough to wrap around your head. Decorate with markers and plastic gems; then staple the ends together. Remember that although this crown may not last, Jesus has promised you a crown that will last forever.

God Always Gives Grace

Our questions betray our lack of understanding:

How can God be everywhere at one time? (Who says God is bound by a body?)

How can God hear all the prayers which come to him? (Perhaps his ears are different from yours.)

How can God be the Father, the Son, and the Holy Spirit? (Could it be that heaven has a different set of physics than earth?)

If people down here won't forgive me, how much more am I guilty before a holy God? (Oh, just the opposite. God is always able to give grace when we humans can't—he invented it.)

The Great House of God

Read Together

"For God all things are possible."

MARK 10:27

20

Questions

The questions that we ask show the things that we do not understand. Maybe you have questions such as these:

How can God be everywhere at one time? *God does not live in a body like yours, so he can do things that your body cannot do.*

How can God hear all the prayers of all the people? *Maybe his ears are different from yours.*

How can God be the Father, the Son, *and* the Holy Spirit—all at once? *Could it be that the natural laws of heaven are different from those of earth?*

If people down here on earth won't forgive me, how could God ever forgive me? *God is always able to forgive—to give you his grace—even when people can't or won't. He can always give you his grace because he invented it.*

GROWING IN GRACE

Do you have a question about God? Take it to your mom or dad, a teacher, preacher, or youth minister. Ask them to help you look through the Bible for an answer. God's Word is always the best place to look for answers!

See What God Has Done!

How vital that we pray, armed with the knowledge that God is in heaven. Pray with any lesser conviction and your prayers are timid, shallow, and hollow. But spend some time walking in the workshop of the heavens, seeing what God has done, and watch how your prayers are energized. . . .

Behold the sun! Every square yard of the sun is constantly emitting 130,000 horsepower, or the equivalent of 450 eight-cylinder automobile engines. And yet our sun, as powerful as it is, is but one minor star in the 100 billion orbs which make up our Milky Way Galaxy. Hold a dime in your fingers and extend it arm's length toward the sky, allowing it to eclipse your vision, and you will block out fifteen million stars from your view. . . . By showing us the heavens, Jesus is showing us his Father's workshop. . . . He taps us on the shoulder and says, "Your Father can handle that for you."

The Great House of God

Read Together

The heavens declare the glory of God.

PSALM 19:1

See What God Has Done!

It is important to pray. But it's just as important to believe that God is in heaven and answers your prayers. To pray without believing makes your prayers weak. If you're having trouble believing, spend some time looking up at the sun, moon, and stars. They show the power and majesty of God. Just look and see the great things that he has done!

Think about the sun. Every square yard of it gives off the power of more than 450 car engines. And yet our sun—as powerful as it is—is just one small star out of the 100 billion stars that make up our Milky Way Galaxy. Hold a dime in your fingers and stretch your arm toward the night sky. That small dime blocks over 15 million stars from your view!

By showing us the heavens, Jesus is showing us his Father's awesomeness. It's as if Jesus is tapping you on the shoulder and saying, "Your Father made all of that, so you can believe that he can take care of you."

GROWING IN GRACE

Check out a book on constellations at the library. Then, on a clear night, take a blanket and lie out under the stars. Can you find the Big Dipper? The Little Dipper? The North Star? How many stars can you count? Remember, the God who knows each of those stars also knows you!

Good Habits

I like the story of the little boy who fell out of bed. When his mom asked him what happened, he answered, "I don't know. I guess I stayed too close to where I got in."

Easy to do the same with our faith. It's tempting just to stay where we got in and never move.

Pick a time in the not-too-distant past. A year or two ago. Now ask yourself a few questions. How does your prayer life today compare with then? How about your giving? Have both the amount and the joy increased? What about your church loyalty? Can you tell you've grown? And Bible study? Are you learning to learn? . . .

Don't make the mistake of the little boy. Don't stay too close to where you got in. It's risky resting on the edge.

When God Whispers Your Name

Read Together

So let us go on to grown-up teaching. Let us not go back over the beginning lessons we learned about Christ.

HEBREWS 6:1

Good Habits

I like the story of the little boy who fell out of bed. When his mom asked him what happened, he answered, "I don't know. I guess I stayed too close to where I got in."

It's easy to do the same thing with your faith. It's easy to just stay where you are. But just as you are growing taller and learning more in school, this is also the time to grow and learn in Christ. Start some habits of faith such as these:

- Pray every day—not just a quick word at mealtime, but really talk to God and tell him about your day.
- Read at least one verse of Scripture every day.
- Memorize a verse each week.
- Go to church and Bible study.
- Decide to do one good thing for someone else each day.

Don't make the mistake of the little boy. Don't stay too close to where you got in. Jump right in, and start growing your faith!

GROWING IN GRACE

As you grow up, keep track of your growing faith. On a growth chart, as you mark your physical growth, also note your spiritual growth. Memorize a verse? Write it on the chart with a date. Help someone learn about Jesus? Write it down. See how "tall" your faith can grow.

A Cut Above

The word *holy* means "to separate." The ancestry of the term can be traced back to an ancient word which means "to cut." To be holy, then, is to be a cut above the norm, superior, extraordinary. . . . The Holy One dwells on a different level from the rest of us. What frightens us does not frighten him. What troubles us does not trouble him.

I'm more a landlubber than a sailor, but I've puttered around in a bass boat enough to know the secret for finding land in a storm. . . . You don't aim at another boat. You certainly don't stare at the waves. You set your sights on an object unaffected by the wind—a light on the shore—and go straight toward it. . . .

When you set your sights on our God, you focus on one "a cut above" any storm life may bring. . . . You find peace.

The Great House of God

Read Together

"Be still, and know that I am God."

PSALM 46:10 NIV

26

A Cut Above

The word *holy* means "to separate." The word's meaning can be traced back to ancient times, when it meant "to cut." To be holy, then, is to be a cut above . . . better than the rest . . . extraordinary. That's God. He is a cut above us. What scares us does not scare him. What troubles us does not trouble him.

I'm not a great sailor, but I've been in a fishing boat enough times to know how to find land in a storm. You don't aim at another boat—it might float the wrong way. Don't stare at the waves—they're always moving. Set your sights on something that isn't moved by the wind—like a light on the shore—and go straight toward it.

When life is stormy, don't follow your friends—they might go the wrong way. Don't stare at your troubles—they're always moving. Set your sights on the One who never moves—God. He is "a cut above" any storm.

GROWING IN GRACE

Does it matter what you set your sights on? Try this: Grab a football or soccer ball and pick a distant object (like a tree) as your goal. Throw the ball at the goal, but don't look at it. Look to the right or left. Miss your goal? Try again, this time keeping your eyes on the goal. Better? Always keep your eyes on the goal—and on God!

God's Goodness

Have you noticed that God doesn't ask you to prove that you will put your salary to good use? Have you noticed that God doesn't turn off your oxygen supply when you misuse his gifts? Aren't you glad that God doesn't give you only that which you remember to thank him for? . . .

God's goodness is spurred by his nature, not by our worthiness.

Someone asked an associate of mine, "What biblical precedent do we have to help the poor who have no desire to become Christians?"

My friend responded with one word: "God."

God does it daily, for millions of people.

In the Eye of the Storm

Read Together

The rich and the poor are alike in that the LORD made them all.

PROVERBS 22:2

God's Goodness

Have you noticed that God doesn't ask you to prove that you will put your time to good use? Have you noticed that God doesn't turn off your air supply when you mess up? Aren't you glad that God doesn't give you only the gifts that you remember to thank him for?

God is good to you because God *is* good. That is who he is. He blesses you because of his goodness, not because you are worthy of it.

Someone once asked a friend of mine, "Why should we help the poor who don't even want to be Christians?"

My friend simply answered, "God did."

Would God help those who don't love him? Those who don't even want to know him? Yes! He did it in the Bible, and he still does it every day for millions of people.

GROWING IN GRACE

God blesses even those who don't like him. That can be a tough thing for us to do. Can you bless someone who doesn't like you? Can you smile at the grouch? Offer to help the grumpy neighbor? You might just make a new friend.

Godless Living

Since the hedonist has never seen the hand who made the universe, he assumes there is no life beyond the here and now. He believes there is no truth beyond this room. No purpose beyond his own pleasure. No divine factor. He has no concern for the eternal. . . .

The hedonist says, "Who cares? I may be bad, but so what? What I do is my business." He's more concerned about satisfying his passions than in knowing the Father. His life is so desperate for pleasure that he has no time or room for God.

Is he right? Is it OK to spend our days thumbing our noses at God and living it up?

Paul says, "Absolutely not!"

According to Romans 1, we lose more than stained-glass windows when we dismiss God. We lose our standard, our purpose, and our worship.

In the Grip of Grace

Read Together

Their thinking became useless. Their foolish minds were filled with darkness. They said they were wise, but they became fools.

ROMANS 1:21–22

Life Without God

There are people who live only to make themselves happy. And because they have never seen God in person, they believe there is no life except the here and now. To them, nothing is real except what they can see. Nothing is important except their own happiness, and there is no Creator and no heaven.

These people say, "Who cares? I may be bad, but so what? What I do is my own business." They are more concerned with having fun than knowing the Father. They are so busy chasing after good times that they have no time for God.

Are they right? Is it okay to spend our days ignoring God and thinking only of ourselves? Absolutely not!

Paul told us in Romans 1 that when we ignore God, we lose more than church on Sundays. We lose the very reason we were created.

GROWING IN GRACE

Many people don't believe that God is real or that he cares. It can be tough to share God's Word with them. But one thing they can't ignore is the way you live. Live like Jesus did—loving others more than yourself. Then God's message will come through loud and clear.

Only One Thing Counts

Think about the day Christ comes. There you are in the great circle of the redeemed. . . . Though you are one of a throng, it's as if you and Jesus are all alone. . . .

I'm speculating now, but I wonder if Christ might say these words to you: "I'm so proud that you let me use you. Because of you, others are here today. Would you like to meet them?" . . .

At that point Jesus might turn to the crowd and invite them. . . . One by one, they begin to step out and walk forward.

The first is your neighbor, a crusty old sort who lived next door. To be frank, you didn't expect to see him. "You never knew I was watching," he explains, "but I was. And because of you, I am here." . . .

It's not long before you and your Savior are encircled by the delightful collection of souls you've touched. Some you know, most you don't, but for each you feel the same. . . . You feel what Paul felt . . . "I'm so proud of your faith" (see 1 Thessalonians 2:19).

When Christ Comes

Read Together

No one has ever imagined what God has prepared for those who love him.

1 CORINTHIANS 2:9

Because of You

Think about the day Jesus comes back. There you are in heaven surrounded by all the other Christians who were saved. Though you are one of a crowd, it's as if you and Jesus are all alone.

I wonder if Jesus might say these words to you: "I'm so proud that you let me use you. Because of you, others are here today. Would you like to meet them?"

And, one by one, they begin to step forward.

The first is that grouchy old lady who lived next door. You didn't think you would see her in heaven! "You never knew I was watching when you did kind things for everyone in the neighborhood," she says, "but I was. And because of you, I am here."

It's not long before you and Jesus are surrounded by all the souls you've touched. Some you know, and some you don't. But you are so happy for each of them. And how wonderful to hear Jesus say, "I am so proud of your faith" (see 1 Thessalonians 2:19).

GROWING IN GRACE

Someone's always watching what you do—even if you don't know it. So . . . are you the one who cheats on the test? The one who lies about the broken glass? Or are you the one who cleans up the mess you didn't make? The one who picks up the trash from the neighbor's yard? Who are you when no one is watching?

Boldness Before the Throne

Jesus tells us, "When you pray, pray like this. 'Our Father which art in heaven, Hallowed be thy name. Thy kingdom come'" (Matthew 6:9–10 KJV).

When you say, "Thy kingdom come," you are inviting the Messiah himself to walk into your world. "Come, my King! Take your throne in our land. Be present in my heart. Be present in my office. Come into my marriage. Be Lord of my family, my fears, and my doubts." This is no feeble request; it's a bold appeal for God to occupy every corner of your life.

And who are you to ask such a thing? Who are you to ask God to take control of your world? You are his child, for heaven's sake! And so you ask boldly.

The Great House of God

Read Together

Let us, then, feel very sure that we can come before God's throne where there is grace.

HEBREWS 4:16

A Bold Prayer

Jesus said, "When you pray, you should pray like this: 'Our Father in heaven, we pray that your name will always be kept holy. We pray that your kingdom will come'" (Matthew 6:9–10 ICB).

When you say, "We pray that your kingdom will come," you are inviting God himself to walk into your world. You are asking him to be the Lord of your life—your entire life. You are saying that you want his will to rule in your heart. That you want everything you say and do to be pleasing to him. That you want him to guide your relationships with your family and friends. And you want him to take charge of your doubts and fears.

This is no small prayer. You are boldly and bravely asking God to come into every corner of your life.

And who are you to ask such a thing? Who are you to ask God to take control of your world? *You are his child!*

GROWING IN GRACE

The next time you're not sure what to pray, find the Lord's Prayer in Matthew 6:9–13. Jesus prayed for God's kingdom to come and his will to be done, for daily needs, for forgiveness, and for protection from the evil one. Practice praying like Jesus did.

Sole Provider, Sole Comforter

As long as Jesus is one of many options, he is no option.

As long as you can carry your burdens alone, you don't need a burden bearer. As long as your situation brings you no grief, you will receive no comfort. And as long as you can take him or leave him, you might as well leave him, because he won't be taken halfheartedly.

But when you mourn, when you get to the point of sorrow for your sins, when you admit that you have no other option but to cast all your cares on him, and when there is truly no other name that you can call, then cast all your cares on him, for he is waiting in the midst of the storm.

The Applause of Heaven

Read Together

"Come to me, all of you who are tired and have heavy loads, and I will give you rest."

MATTHEW 11:28

Only Jesus

As long as Jesus is just one of many choices, you probably won't choose him.

As long as you think you can handle all of your problems by yourself, you don't need a problem-fixer. As long as you are feeling happy, you don't need comfort. As long as you would rather follow your friends Monday through Saturday and follow Jesus only on Sunday, you're not really following him at all. Because he wants all of you every day, not just a little bit on Sunday.

But when you realize that you have sinned and your heart breaks because of your sins, Jesus will be waiting for you. When you are ready to give him all your worries and cares, he will be there. When your problems flash around you like lightning in a storm, Jesus will be right there in the middle of the storm— waiting to save you.

GROWING IN GRACE

Some substitutes are okay—like margarine for butter. But others aren't. Try this: stir up a package of powdered drink mix, but use flour instead of sugar. Did it work? No! Faith is the same way. Some people put their faith in money, friends, or fame, but there's no substitute for Jesus!

Led by the Spirit

To hear many of us talk, you'd think we were confused about God's Spirit. You'd think we didn't believe in the Trinity. We talk about the Father and study the Son—but when it comes to the Holy Spirit, we are confused at best and frightened at worst. Confused because we've never been taught. Frightened because we've been taught to be afraid.

May I simplify things a bit? The Holy Spirit is the presence of God in our lives, carrying on the work of Jesus. The Holy Spirit helps us in three directions—inwardly (by granting us the fruit of the Spirit, Galatians 5:22–24), upwardly (by praying for us, Romans 8:26), and outwardly (by pouring God's love into our hearts, Romans 5:5).

When God Whispers Your Name

Read Together

The true children of God are those who let God's Spirit lead them.

ROMANS 8:14

The Holy Spirit

You hear a lot of people talk about God and about Jesus. But when it comes to the Holy Spirit, nobody says much. And sometimes the thought of a "spirit" can be confusing, maybe even frightening. But the truth is, we're confused because no one has taught us about him. And we're frightened because we don't understand him.

Let's make things a bit simpler. The Holy Spirit is nothing to be afraid of—he is a gift from God. He is the presence of God living inside us, and he carries on the work of Jesus in our lives.

The Holy Spirit works in three ways: he helps our hearts by giving us the fruit of the Spirit (Galatians 5:22–24). He prays to God for us when we don't know what to say (Romans 8:26). And he pours God's love into our hearts (5:5).

The Holy Spirit is God living in you—and that is nothing to be frightened of!

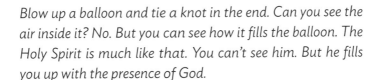

GROWING IN GRACE

Blow up a balloon and tie a knot in the end. Can you see the air inside it? No. But you can see how it fills the balloon. The Holy Spirit is much like that. You can't see him. But he fills you up with the presence of God.

God Is Crazy About You

There are many reasons God saves you: to bring glory to himself, to appease his justice, to demonstrate his sovereignty. But one of the sweetest reasons God saved you is because he is fond of you. He likes having you around. He thinks you are the best thing to come down the pike in quite a while. . . .

If God had a refrigerator, your picture would be on it. If he had a wallet, your photo would be in it. He sends you flowers every spring and a sunrise every morning. Whenever you want to talk, he'll listen. He can live anywhere in the universe, and he chose your heart. . . .

Face it, friend. He's crazy about you.

A Gentle Thunder

Read Together

"God even knows how many hairs are on your head."

MATTHEW 10:30

Crazy About You

There are many reasons God saves you. It brings glory to him. It allows you to come to him without any sin. It shows that he is Lord of all. But one of the sweetest reasons God saves you is because he is *fond* of you. He likes having you around. He thinks you are the best thing to come along since peanut butter.

If God had a refrigerator, your picture would be on it. If he had a wallet, your photo would be in it. He sends you flowers every spring and a sunrise every morning. Whenever you want to talk, he listens. God can live anywhere in the universe—the highest mountain or the most beautiful beach. But he chooses to live in your heart.

Face it, friend. God is crazy about you!

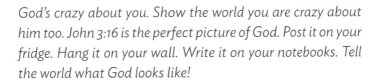

GROWING IN GRACE

God's crazy about you. Show the world you are crazy about him too. John 3:16 is the perfect picture of God. Post it on your fridge. Hang it on your wall. Write it on your notebooks. Tell the world what God looks like!

A Burst of Love

Sometimes God is so touched by what he sees that he gives us what we need and not simply that for which we ask.

It's a good thing. For who would have ever thought to ask God for what he gives? Which of us would have dared to say: "God, would you please hang yourself on a tool of torture as a substitution for every mistake I have ever committed?" And then have the audacity to add: "And after you forgive me, could you prepare me a place in your house to live forever?"

And if that wasn't enough: "And would you please live within me and protect me and guide me and bless me with more than I could ever deserve?"

Honestly, would we have the chutzpah to ask for that? . . .

Jesus already knows the cost of grace. He already knows the price of forgiveness. But he offers it anyway. Love burst his heart.

He Still Moves Stones

Read Together

"Seek God's kingdom, and your other needs will be met as well."

Luke 12:31

Who Would Ask?

God loves us so much that he doesn't just give us the things we ask him for—like good health and help with family and school. God also gives us what we need—a Savior.

And that's a good thing. For who would ever dare to say, "God, would you please take away all my sins and mistakes by hanging yourself from a wooden cross?" Who would dare to add, "And after you forgive me, could you prepare a place in your house for me to live forever?"

And if that weren't enough, would you have ever thought to ask, "God, would you please live in my heart and protect me and guide me and bless me with more than I could ever imagine or deserve?"

Honestly, would we have the nerve to ask for that?

Jesus already knows the price of forgiving us. He already knows the cost of grace. But he gives us his grace anyway.

GROWING IN GRACE

To help you know how much God loves you, write John 3:16 (ICB) on an index card. Fill in your name in the spaces shown: "For God loved [your name] so much that he gave his only Son. God gave his Son so that [your name] whoever believes in him may not be lost, but have eternal life."

Listen for His Voice

Let me state something important. There is never a time during which Jesus is not speaking. Never. There is never a place in which Jesus is not present. Never. There is never a room so dark . . . a lounge so sensual . . . an office so sophisticated . . . that the ever-present, ever-pursuing, relentlessly tender Friend is not there, tapping gently on the doors of our hearts—waiting to be invited in.

Few hear his voice. Fewer still open the door.

But never interpret our numbness as his absence. For amidst the fleeting promises of pleasure is the timeless promise of his presence.

"Surely I am with you always, to the very end of the age" (Matthew 28:20 NIV). . . .

There is no chorus so loud that the voice of God cannot be heard . . . if we will but listen.

In the Eye of the Storm

Read Together

"Never will I leave you;
    never will I forsake you."

HEBREWS 13:5 NIV

44

Listen for His Voice

Let me tell you something very important. There is never a time that Jesus is not speaking. *Never*. There is never a place where Jesus isn't there. *Never*. There is never a room so dark that your greatest Friend is not around. He is always present, always seeking, always tender. It's as if he is gently tapping on the door of your heart—just waiting to be invited in.

Not many people hear his voice. Even fewer people open the door of their hearts to him.

But that doesn't mean he isn't there. Because he is. He promised he always would be: "You can be sure that I will be with you always. I will continue with you until the end of the world" (Matthew 28:20 ICB).

Some people in this world may tell you to stop listening to Jesus. They may tell you that the things he says are wrong aren't really wrong. Don't listen to them. Open up your Bible and listen for Jesus' voice. His Word will speak to you . . . if you will listen.

GROWING IN GRACE

Some mornings can be pretty chilly. Use those chilly mornings to help you remember that God is everywhere. Breathe out and notice the white, puffy clouds. We usually don't see the air, but the cold lets us see it. And just like the air, God is everywhere—even though we don't see him.

God Hears Our Prayers

When [a friend] told Jesus of the illness [of Lazarus] he said, "Lord, the one you love is sick" (John 11:3). He doesn't base his appeal on the imperfect love of the one in need, but on the perfect love of the Savior. He doesn't say, "The one *who loves you* is sick." He says, "The one *you love* is sick." The power of the prayer, in other words, does not depend on the one who makes the prayer, but on the one who hears the prayer.

We can and must repeat the phrase in manifold ways. "The one you love is tired, sad, hungry, lonely, fearful, depressed." The words of the prayer vary, but the response never changes. The Savior hears the prayer. He silences heaven, so he won't miss a word. He hears the prayer.

The Great House of God

Read Together

The LORD hears good people when they cry out to him,
and he saves them from all their troubles.

PSALM 34:17

Jesus Hears Your Prayers

When a friend came to Jesus and told him that Lazarus was sick, he said, "Lord, the one you love is sick" (John 11:3 ICB).

The man didn't come to Jesus and talk about Lazarus's imperfect love for Jesus. He didn't say, "The one *who loves you* is sick." No. He reminded Jesus of his perfect love for Lazarus. He said, "The one *you love* is sick."

When you talk to Jesus in prayer, the power of the prayer is not in you, the one who says the prayer. The power is in the One who hears the prayer.

So when you pray, you can use the same words as Lazarus's friend: "The one you love is sick . . . tired . . . sad . . . hungry . . . lonely . . . afraid." You can pray this way, because *you* are the one Jesus loves.

The words of your prayers may change, but what Jesus does never changes. Your Savior never misses a word. He hears your prayer.

GROWING IN GRACE

Listening to your prayers is just one way Jesus shows his love. Keep a journal this week. Write down all the different ways that Jesus says, "I love you." From the sunrise painted just for you . . . to the air you breathe . . . to the stars that sparkle in the sky.

Dark Nights—God's Light

You wonder if it is a blessing or a curse to have a mind that never rests. But you would rather be a cynic than a hypocrite, so you continue to pray with one eye open and wonder:

> about starving children
> about the power of prayer
> about Christians in cancer wards . . .

Tough questions. Throw-in-the-towel questions. Questions the disciples must have asked in the storm.

All they could see were black skies as they bounced in the battered boat. . . .

Then a figure came to them walking on the water. It wasn't what they expected. . . . They almost missed seeing the answer to their prayers.

And unless we look and listen closely, we risk making the same mistake. God's lights in our dark nights are as numerous as the stars, if only we'll look for them.

In the Eye of the Storm

Read Together

Pray for all people, asking God for what they need and being thankful to him.

1 TIMOTHY 2:1

Dark Nights, God's Light

Do you ever look at the world around you and wonder about some of the things that happen here? As you pray, do you ever wonder about things like . . . starving children, Christians with cancer, and why bad things happen to God's people?

Those are tough questions. They are probably a lot like the questions the disciples must have asked when they were in the middle of the sea during a storm: "Jesus, don't you care?"

All they could see were black skies and black waves as they bounced in the battered boat. Then a figure came to them, walking on the water. It wasn't what they expected, so they almost missed seeing the answer to their prayers.

And unless you look and listen closely, you might make the same mistake. God's answers are like the stars in the night sky—there are billions and billions of them. But some of them you just can't see yet.

GROWING IN GRACE

God often uses his children—that's you!—as answers to tough questions. His children can feed the hungry. His children can visit the hospitals. And his children can comfort the hurting. Ask God what you can do to help others. You just might be the answer to someone's tough question.

God's Child

Let me tell you who you are. In fact, let me proclaim who you are.

You are an heir of God and a co-heir with Christ (Romans 8:17).
You are eternal, like an angel (Luke 20:36).
You have a crown that will last forever (1 Corinthians 9:25).
You are a holy priest (1 Peter 2:5), a treasured possession
(Exodus 19:5). . . .

But more than any of the above—more significant than any title
or position—is the simple fact that you are God's child. . . .

"We really are his children."

As a result, if something is important to you, it's important
to God.

He Still Moves Stones

Read Together

The Father has loved us so much that we are called children of
God. And we really are his children.

1 JOHN 3:1

God's Child

Do you know who you are? Let me tell you:

You are the brother or sister of Christ (Romans 8:17).
You are eternal—you will never die—just like the angels (Luke 20:36).
You have a crown that will last forever (1 Corinthians 9:25).
You are his treasured possession (Exodus 19:5).

But more than any of those things—more important than any title—is the simple fact that you are God's own child.

"We really are his children," and *you* really are his child.

And because you are his child, if something is important to you, it's important to God.

GROWING IN GRACE

There is no problem too small to take to God. No worry, no mistake, no joy. Nothing is too small to pray about. God wants to hear it all—no matter what it is. If it's important to you, then it's important to God.

A Meeting of Moments

The cross was no accident.

Jesus' death was not the result of a panicking cosmological engineer. The cross wasn't a tragic surprise. Calvary was not a knee-jerk response to a world plummeting toward destruction. It wasn't a patch-up job or a stopgap measure. The death of the Son of God was anything but an unexpected peril.

No, it was part of an incredible plan. A calculated choice.

The moment the forbidden fruit touched the lips of Eve, the shadow of a cross appeared on the horizon. And between that moment and the moment the man with the mallet placed the spike against the wrist of God, a master plan was fulfilled.

God Came Near

Read Together

[They] put him to death by nailing him to a cross. But this was God's plan which he had made long ago.

ACTS 2:23

52

An Incredible Plan

The cross didn't just happen.

Jesus' death was not an accident. The cross wasn't a sad surprise. Calvary was not some cosmic mix-up or galactic goof. It wasn't some failed attempt to save the world. Jesus' death was anything but unexpected.

No, Jesus' death was part of God's incredible plan to save you, to save me, and to save all of his children. And that plan started thousands of years before Jesus came to earth.

The moment that forbidden fruit touched the lips of Eve, God had a plan to save us all. Although the cross wouldn't appear for centuries, the plan for it began in the Garden of Eden. And between that moment in the garden and the moment the first nail went into the cross, God's great plan to save us was fulfilled.

GROWING IN GRACE

April 1 is called April Fools' Day. And one day, more than two thousand years ago, Satan became the biggest fool of all. When Jesus died on the cross, Satan thought he had won. But—April Fool!—Jesus rose from the grave, and the devil lost forever.

You Were in His Prayers

The final prayer of Jesus was about you. His final pain was for you. His final passion was for you. Before he went to the cross, Jesus went to the garden. And when he spoke with his Father, you were in his prayers. . . .

And God couldn't turn his back on you. He couldn't because he saw you, and one look at you was all it took to convince him. Right there in the middle of a world which isn't fair. He saw you cast into a river of life you didn't request. He saw you betrayed by those you love. He saw you with a body which gets sick and a heart which grows weak. . . .

On the eve of the cross, Jesus made his decision. He would rather go to hell for you than go to heaven without you.

And the Angels Were Silent

Read Together

Then Jesus went about a stone's throw away from them. He kneeled down and prayed.

Luke 22:41

Jesus Prayed for You

In the Garden of Gethsemane, Jesus prayed about many things. But did you know that he also prayed about you? Jesus loved you so much that—in his last hours on earth—he just had to talk to God about you. He prayed that you would be with him and that you would see his glory (John 17:24). And he prayed that God would keep you safe from the evils of this world (John 17:11).

And today, more than two thousand years later, God is still answering Jesus' prayer. He knows the troubles you face, the tough decisions, and even the temptations to do wrong. He knows your every struggle to do the right thing, your every sadness, and your every joy. And he promises that he will always be right there with you to help you through (Matthew 28:20).

GROWING IN GRACE

On the night before he died, Jesus took time to pray for you. Read John 17:6–26. Make a list of all the things Jesus asked God to bless you with. Do you know someone who does not know Jesus? Be like Jesus and pray for that person.

The Worshipful Heart

Worship. In two thousand years we haven't worked out the kinks. We still struggle for the right words in prayer. We still fumble over Scripture. We don't know when to kneel. We don't know when to stand. We don't know how to pray.

Worship is a daunting task.

For that reason, God gave us the Psalms—a praise book for God's people. . . . This collection of hymns and petitions are strung together by one thread—a heart hungry for God.

Some are defiant. Others are reverent. Some are to be sung. Others are to be prayed. Some are intensely personal. Others are written as if the whole world would use them. . . .

The very variety should remind us that worship is personal. No secret formula exists. What moves you may stymie another. Each worships differently. But each should worship.

The Inspirational Study Bible

Read Together

Come, let's worship him and bow down.
Let's kneel before the LORD who made us.

PSALM 95:6

Worship from the Heart

Worship. In two thousand years we still haven't figured it out. We still struggle with the right words to pray. We don't know when to kneel. We don't know when to stand. We don't know how to pray.

Worship can be confusing.

That's why God gave us Psalms: to help us worship him. It is a praise book for God's people. And although the psalms talk about many different things, they each have the same purpose: to draw us closer to the heart of God.

Some psalms are bold. Others are humble. Some are to be sung. Others are to be prayed. Some seem written just for you alone. Others seem to be for the whole world to sing.

The fact that there are so many different kinds of psalms reminds us that there are many different kinds of worship. There is no one secret formula, no one right way. Each person worships differently. But each person should worship.

GROWING IN GRACE

Take a stroll through the book of Psalms. Look at all the different titles, such as A Prayer for Protection (Psalm 140), A Song of Trust in God (Psalm 27), and God in the Thunderstorm (Psalm 29). When you don't know what to pray, turn to the psalms.

His Broken Heart

I can't understand it. I honestly cannot. Why did Jesus [die on the cross]? Oh, I know, I know. I have heard the official answers. "To gratify the old law." "To fulfill prophecy." And these answers are right. They are. But there is something more here. Something very compassionate. Something yearning. Something personal.

What is it?

Could it be that his heart was broken for all the people who cast despairing eyes toward the dark heavens and cry the same "Why?" Could it be that his heart was broken for the hurting? . . .

I imagine him, bending close to those who hurt. I imagine him listening. I picture his eyes misting and a pierced hand brushing away a tear. . . . He who also was once alone, understands.

No Wonder They Call Him the Savior

Read Together

When he saw the crowds, he felt sorry for them because they were hurting and helpless, like sheep without a shepherd.

MATTHEW 9:36

Jesus' Broken Heart

Think of all the different people who came to Jesus for help. All kinds of people. Young children and old beggars. The sick and the lame. The kind and the selfish. It seems that everywhere Jesus went, great crowds of people came to him, wanting his help.

Surely there must have been times when he was tired, when he just wanted to rest. Why didn't he simply turn them away and tell them to come back tomorrow? Why didn't he take a day off now and then? Why?

Could it be that Jesus' heart hurt for those people? Could it be that his heart was—and is—broken for all people who have ever stared up at the heavens and cried out in prayer, "Why is this happening to me?"

Imagine Jesus today: he is leaning over, bending down close to someone who is hurt. He's listening. His eyes fill with tears as he hears that person's troubles. Then his hand gently brushes away a tear. He was hurt once too. He understands.

GROWING IN GRACE

Jesus is never too busy to listen to your prayers. Do you find yourself too busy for others sometimes? The next time your friends need you to listen or to help, take time for them. It's what Jesus would do.

A Holy Task

Mary and Mary[Magdalene knew a task had to be done—Jesus' body had to be prepared for burial. Peter didn't offer to do it. Andrew didn't volunteer. . . . So the two Marys decide to do it. . . .

I wonder if halfway to the tomb they had sat down and reconsidered. What if they'd looked at each other and shrugged, "What's the use?" What if they had given up? What if one had thrown up her arms in frustration and bemoaned, "I'm tired of being the only one who cares. Let Andrew do something for a change. Let Nathaniel show some leadership."

Whether or not they were tempted to, I'm glad they didn't quit. That would have been tragic. You see, we know something they didn't. We know the Father was watching. Mary and Mary thought they were alone. They weren't. They thought their journey was unnoticed. They were wrong. God knew.

He Still Moves Stones

Read Together

Everything you do or say should be done to obey Jesus your Lord.

Colossians 3:17

God Still Knows

Mary and Mary Magdalene knew what needed to be done. Jesus' body needed to be anointed—or covered—with special spices before he could be buried. That's what the Jews did for people who had died. And it was the last thing that the women could do for their Lord. Peter didn't offer to do it. Andrew didn't volunteer to do it. So the two Marys decided to do it (Mark 16:1–2).

What would have happened if, on the way to the tomb, they had changed their minds? What if they had given up? What if one had thrown up her hands and moaned, "I'm tired of being the only one who cares. Let Andrew do something for a change. Let Nathanael take a turn"?

It would have been so sad if they had given up and decided to quit. You see, we know something they didn't. We know the Father was watching. Mary and Mary thought they were alone. They weren't. They thought no one knew about their journey. They were wrong. God knew—just as he knows all the good that you do.

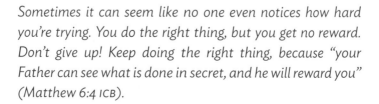

GROWING IN GRACE

Sometimes it can seem like no one even notices how hard you're trying. You do the right thing, but you get no reward. Don't give up! Keep doing the right thing, because "your Father can see what is done in secret, and he will reward you" (Matthew 6:4 ICB).

Insufficient Funds

If Christ had not covered us with his grace, each of us would be overdrawn on [our heavenly bank] account. When it comes to goodness we would have insufficient funds. Inadequate holiness. God requires a certain balance of virtue in our account, and it's more than any of us has alone. Our holiness account shows insufficient funds, and only the holy will see the Lord; what can we do?

We could try making a few deposits. Maybe if I wave at my neighbor or compliment my husband or go to church next Sunday, I'll get caught up. But how do you know when you've made enough? . . .

If you are trying to justify your own statement, forget ever having peace. . . . You are trying to justify an account you can't justify. . . . "It is God who justifies" (Romans 8:33).

The Great House of God

Read Together

People cannot do any work that will make them right with God.

Romans 4:5

Never Enough

Pretend you have a bank account in heaven—a "holiness account."

In order to get into heaven, your holiness account must be full. So you try to fill your account by doing as many good things as you can. Maybe you say something nice to a friend, or help your neighbor rake up leaves, or help out in the church nursery. Maybe you lead prayers or memorize Bible verses. Surely doing more good things will earn you some extra holiness, right? That should fill up your holiness account, right?

Wrong. When it comes to goodness, you can never do enough. You can never earn enough holiness. To get to heaven, God demands that your holiness account be full—and you just can't do that on your own. So how *do* you get to heaven? Jesus.

When you choose to believe in Jesus and to obey him, he fills up your holiness account for you. It's called *grace*—and it's his gift to you.

GROWING IN GRACE

You simply can't earn your way to heaven. It is a gift from God. Your gift to God is worship. Make up your own song of worship and praise to God, thanking him for his gift.

The Fire of Your Heart

Want to know God's will for your life? Then answer this question: What ignites your heart? Forgotten orphans? Untouched nations? The inner city? The outer limits?

Heed the fire within!

Do you have a passion to sing? Then sing! Are you stirred to manage? Then manage! Do you ache for the ill? Then treat them! Do you hurt for the lost? Then teach them!

As a young man I felt the call to preach. Unsure if I was correct in my reading of God's will for me, I sought the counsel of a minister I admired. His counsel still rings true. "Don't preach," he said, "unless you have to."

As I pondered his words I found my answer: "I have to. If I don't, the fire will consume me."

What is the fire that consumes you?

The Great House of God

Read Together

My God, I want to do what you want.
Your teachings are in my heart.

PSALM 40:8

64

The Fire in Your Heart

Want to know God's will for your life? Then answer this question: What sets your heart on fire? That is, what do you feel that you just *have to do* to show God's love or to help others? Is it helping orphans? Or the homeless? Or people who don't know Jesus?

Pay attention to the fire in your heart! Do you love to sing more than anything? Then sing! Does your heart hurt for the sick and the lonely? Then comfort them!

As a young man, I felt that God wanted me to preach. But I wasn't sure if I understood God's will correctly. So I talked to a minister whom I looked up to. His advice to me was, "Don't preach unless you *have* to."

As I thought about his words, I found my answer. "I have to preach. If I don't, this fire in my heart will burn me up. If I don't preach, I'll spend the rest of my life wishing that I had."

What is the fire in your heart? What is it that you just *have to do* for God?

GROWING IN GRACE

Make a list of all the things that you love to do. Do you love to play ball? To sing? Do crafts? Paint or read? Ask God to show you how you can worship him and share his Word by using the things you love to do.

A Cleared Calendar

How long has it been since you let God have you?

I mean really *have* you? How long since you gave him a portion of undiluted, uninterrupted time listening for his voice? Apparently, Jesus did. He made a deliberate effort to spend time with God.

Spend much time reading about the listening life of Jesus and a distinct pattern emerges. He spent regular time with God, praying and listening. Mark says, "Very early in the morning, while it was still dark, Jesus got up, left the house and went off to a solitary place, where he prayed" (Mark 1:35 NIV). . . .

Let me ask the obvious. If Jesus, the Son of God, the sinless Savior of humankind, thought it worthwhile to clear his calendar to pray, wouldn't we be wise to do the same?

Just Like Jesus

Read Together

Jesus often withdrew to lonely places and prayed.

LUKE 5:16 NIV

Time Just for God

How long has it been since you let God have your full attention?

I mean *really* have all of your attention. How long since you gave him a part of your day—without any computers or television or telephones? How long since you just listened for his voice and did nothing else? That's what Jesus did. He set aside time to spend time with God—just God.

If you read about the life of Jesus in the Bible, you'll see that he made time with God a habit. He spent time with God regularly, praying and listening. Mark said, "Early the next morning, Jesus woke and left the house while it was still dark. He went to a place to be alone and pray" (Mark 1:35 ICB).

Let me ask you a question. If Jesus—the Son of God, the Savior who never sinned—thought he needed to take time to pray, wouldn't we be smart to do the same?

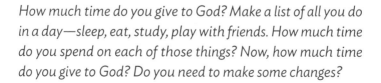

GROWING IN GRACE

How much time do you give to God? Make a list of all you do in a day—sleep, eat, study, play with friends. How much time do you spend on each of those things? Now, how much time do you give to God? Do you need to make some changes?

Character Creates Courage

A legend from India tells about a mouse who was terrified of cats until a magician agreed to transform him into a cat. That resolved his fear . . . until he met a dog, so the magician changed him into a dog. The mouse-turned-cat-turned-dog was content until he met a tiger—so, once again, the magician changed him into what he feared. But when the tiger came complaining that he had met a hunter, the magician refused to help. "I will make you into a mouse again, for though you have the body of a tiger, you still have the heart of a mouse."

Sound familiar? How many people do you know who have built a formidable exterior, only to tremble inside with fear? . . . We face our fears with force . . . or . . . we stockpile wealth. We seek security in things. We cultivate fame and seek status.

But do these approaches work?

Courage is an outgrowth of who we are. Exterior supports may temporarily sustain, but only inward character creates courage.

The Applause of Heaven

Read Together

All you who put your hope in the LORD
be strong and brave.

PSALM 31:24

Courage

A legend from India tells about a mouse who was terrified of cats until a magician agreed to change him into a cat. That fixed his fear . . . until he met a dog. So the magician changed him into a dog. The mouse-turned-cat-turned-dog was happy . . . until he met a tiger. So, once again, the magician changed him into what he feared. But when the tiger came complaining that he had met a hunter, the magician would not help. "I will make you into a mouse again, for even though you have the body of a tiger, you still have the heart of a mouse."

Like that tiger, lots of people look big and tough on the outside, but inside they are trembling with fear. We fight our fears, and we try to make ourselves safe by wearing the right clothes, hanging out with the right friends, and having the right stuff. But does that really work? Are we any less frightened?

Courage comes from who we are inside—God's children—not what we have on the outside.

GROWING IN GRACE

God is your "rock and [your] protection" (Psalm 31:3 ICB). Head out to a park. Find the biggest rock you can and hide behind it. Can anything get to you through that rock? God is even stronger than that rock. Hide yourself in him, and the devil can't touch you!

Sometimes God Says No

Can you imagine the outcome if a parent honored each request of each child during a trip? We'd inch our bloated bellies from one ice-cream store to the next. . . .

Can you imagine the chaos if God indulged each of ours? . . .

"For God has not *destined* us [emphasis mine] to the terrors of judgement, but to the full attainment of salvation through our Lord Jesus Christ" (1 Thessalonians 5:9 NEB).

Note God's destiny for your life. Salvation.

God's overarching desire is that you reach that destiny. His itinerary includes stops that encourage your journey. He frowns on stops that deter you. When his sovereign plan and your earthly plan collide, a decision must be made. Who's in charge of this journey?

If God must choose between your earthly satisfaction and your heavenly salvation, which do you hope he chooses?

Me too.

In the Eye of the Storm

Read Together

Continue praying, keeping alert, and always thanking God.

COLOSSIANS 4:2

70

Sometimes God Says No

Can you imagine what would happen if your parents gave you everything you asked for on your next trip? You'd end up crawling with a bloated belly from one ice-cream store to the next.

Can you imagine the mess there would be if God gave us everything we asked for?

"God did not *choose* us to suffer his anger, but to have salvation through our Lord Jesus Christ" (1 Thessalonians 5:9 ICB, emphasis added).

In this verse, what does it say God chooses for your life? Salvation. God's greatest want is that you reach heaven. His plan includes stops that will help you on your journey to heaven. He frowns on stops that slow you down. When his perfect plan and your earthly plan crash together, a choice must be made. Who's in charge of this journey? You or God?

It's God. And I'm glad he chose heaven for us all.

GROWING IN GRACE

Parents have to say no sometimes. The next time your parents tell you no—before you get upset—stop and think about why they said no. Could it be that saying no was best for you? Want to really shock them? Thank them for caring enough to say no!

God's in Charge

Satan has no power except that which God gives him.

To the first-century church in Smyrna, Christ said, "Do not be afraid of what you are about to suffer. I tell you, the devil will put some of you in prison to test you, and you will suffer for ten days. But be faithful, even if you have to die, and I will give you the crown of life" (Revelation 2:10).

Analyze Jesus' words for a minute. Christ informs the church of the persecution, the duration of the persecution (ten days), the reason for the persecution (to test you), and the outcome of the persecution (a crown of life). In other words, Jesus uses Satan to fortify his church. . . .

Even when [Satan] appears to win, he loses.

The Great House of God

Read Together

God's Spirit, who is in you, is greater than the devil, who is in the world.

1 JOHN 4:4

72

God's in Charge

Sometimes it may seem like Satan is winning the battle for this world and that he is in charge. But God is in *complete* control, and he has an amazing way of using Satan's evil plans to do good. Satan thought he had won when Jesus died on the cross. But God raised Jesus from the dead and gave the gift of salvation to his people.

Many Christians in the early church were thrown in prison or killed. Many others left their homes and ran away to other lands. But God used those hard times to spread his word to other countries. Sad things and even bad things happen to all people—to those who believe in God and those who don't. But God has a special promise for his children: "In everything God works for the good of those who love him" (Romans 8:28 ICB).

When you see sad things or even bad things in your life, when it seems like Satan is winning, remember that God will somehow use those things for good. Because God is in charge.

GROWING IN GRACE

Believing in Jesus can be risky. Some people may laugh at you. You may lose a friend when you refuse to do something wrong that everyone else is doing. Yes, following Jesus has its risks, but the rewards are amazing!

Get Out of the Judgment Seat

We condemn a man for stumbling this morning, but we didn't see the blows he took yesterday. We judge a woman for the limp in her walk, but cannot see the tack in her shoe. We mock the fear in their eyes, but have no idea how many stones they have ducked or darts they have dodged.

Are they too loud? Perhaps they fear being neglected again. Are they too timid? Perhaps they fear failing again. Too slow? Perhaps they fell the last time they hurried. You don't know. Only one who has followed yesterday's steps can be their judge.

Not only are we ignorant about yesterday, we are ignorant about tomorrow. Dare we judge a book while chapters are yet unwritten? Should we pass a verdict on a painting while the artist still holds the brush? How can you dismiss a soul until God's work is complete? "God began doing a good work in you, and I am sure he will continue it until it is finished when Jesus Christ comes again" (Philippians 1:6).

In the Grip of Grace

Read Together

"You will be judged in the same way that you judge others."

MATTHEW 7:2

Who Are You to Judge?

We laugh at the boy who stumbles this morning, but we didn't see how hard he was hit yesterday. We make fun of the girl with the limp, but we cannot see the rock in her shoe.

Is someone too loud? Maybe he is afraid of being ignored again. Is someone else scared? Maybe she is afraid of failing again. Are others moving too slowly? Maybe they fell the last time they ran. We don't know. Only the One who is always watching them can know.

Not only do we not know about their yesterdays, but we don't know about their tomorrows either. We must leave the judging to God. Our job is to "love each other" and to "be kind and humble" to each other (1 Peter 3:8 ICB). Remember, "God began doing a good work in you. And he will continue it until it is finished when Jesus Christ comes again" (Philippians 1:6 ICB). God's not finished with you—or them—yet!

GROWING IN GRACE

Pick up a book that doesn't have any pictures. Can you tell what kind of story is inside? No! People are much the same way. You only see the outside, but the inside is where the story is. Don't judge a book—or a person—by the cover.

A Higher Standard

Most of my life I've been a closet slob. . . . Then I got married. . . .

I enrolled in a twelve-step program for slobs. ("My name is Max, I hate to vacuum.") A physical therapist helped me rediscover the muscles used for hanging shirts. . . . My nose was reintroduced to the fragrance of Pine-Sol. . . .

Then came the moment of truth. Denalyn went out of town for a week. Initially I reverted to the old man. I figured I'd be a slob for six days and clean on the seventh. But something strange happened, a curious discomfort. I couldn't relax with dirty dishes in the sink.

What had happened to me? Simple. I'd been exposed to a higher standard.

Isn't that what has happened with us? . . . Before Christ our lives were out of control, sloppy, and indulgent. We didn't even know we were slobs until we met him. . . . Suddenly we find ourselves wanting to do good. Go back to the old mess? Are you kidding?

In the Grip of Grace

Read Together

I keep trying to reach the goal and get the prize for which God called me.

PHILIPPIANS 3:14

A Better Way

Life at camp is a lot different from life at home. The first day or two, it's great. Nobody cares if you leave your socks on the floor or take a shower or brush your teeth. You can be a total slob, and no one cares.

About the middle of the week, things start to change. You get tired of stepping over your dirty clothes and everyone else's. You really wish you had a clean bed. And that smell you've been smelling—it's you! By the end of the week, you can't take it anymore. Out come the soap and toothpaste, and up go the socks and towels.

What happened? Simple. You knew there was a better way.

Isn't that what Jesus does for us? Before we knew Jesus, our lives were sloppy and selfish. But suddenly now we want to do good—even when no one is looking! Go back to the old mess? Are you kidding? Not a chance. There's a better way.

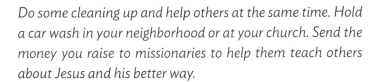

GROWING IN GRACE

Do some cleaning up and help others at the same time. Hold a car wash in your neighborhood or at your church. Send the money you raise to missionaries to help them teach others about Jesus and his better way.

The Correct Solution

At the moment I don't feel too smart. I just got off the wrong plane that took me to the wrong city and left me at the wrong airport. I went east instead of west and ended up in Houston instead of Denver.

It didn't look like the wrong plane, but it was. I walked through the wrong gate, dozed off on the wrong flight, and ended up in the wrong place.

Paul says we've all done the same thing. Not with airplanes and airports, but with our lives and God. He tells the Roman readers,

There is none righteous, no, not one (Romans 3:10 NKJV).

All have sinned and fall short of the glory of God (Romans 3:23 NKJV).

We are all on the wrong plane, he says. All of us. Gentile and Jew. Every person has taken the wrong turn. And we need help. . . . The wrong solutions are pleasure and pride (Romans 1 and 2); the correct solution is Christ Jesus (Romans 3:21–26).

The Inspirational Study Bible

Read Together

The just shall live by faith.

ROMANS 1:17 NKJV

The person who is made right with God by faith will live forever.

ROMANS 1:17 ICB

The Right Answer

At the moment I don't feel too smart. I just got off the wrong plane at the wrong airport in the wrong city. I went east instead of west and ended up in Texas instead of Colorado. Oops.

It didn't look like the wrong plane, but it was. I walked through the wrong gate, fell asleep on the wrong flight, and ended up in the wrong place.

Paul said we've all done the same thing. Not with airplanes and airports, but with our lives and with God. He said: "There is no one without sin. None!" (Romans 3:10 ICB). "All people have sinned and are not good enough for God's glory" (v. 23 ICB).

It's like we are all on the wrong plane. All of us. Boy and girl. Grown-up and child. Every person has taken the wrong turn at some point. And we need help. The wrong answers are selfishness and chasing after fun (Romans 1 and 2). The right answer is Christ Jesus (3:21–26).

GROWING IN GRACE

Visit an airport. Notice how all the planes look pretty much the same. Only certain people know the right one—the people in charge. That's true with a lot of choices. Sometimes bad choices look like good ones. Only the One in charge knows the difference. Check with him before you choose.

God Is Angry at Evil

Many don't understand God's anger because they confuse the wrath of God with the wrath of man. The two have little in common. Human anger is typically self-driven and prone to explosions of temper and violent deeds. We get ticked off because we've been overlooked, neglected, or cheated. This is the anger of man. It is not, however, the anger of God.

God doesn't get angry because he doesn't get his way. He gets angry because disobedience always results in self-destruction. What kind of father sits by and watches his child hurt himself?

In the Grip of Grace

Read Together

So put all evil things out of your life. . . . These things make God angry.

COLOSSIANS 3:5–6

God's Anger

Many people don't understand God's anger. They confuse the anger of God with the anger of people. But the two are very different. People's anger is usually selfish. It shows itself in explosions of temper and violence. We get upset because we've been ignored, skipped over, or cheated. When we don't get what we want, we get mad. This is the anger of people. It is not, however, the anger of God.

God doesn't get angry because he doesn't get his way. He gets angry because we disobey him. And he knows that by disobeying him, we will always end up getting hurt. After all, what kind of father sits by and watches his child hurt himself? Not God!

GROWING IN GRACE

Spend an hour helping in your church's toddler class. Pick out one youngster who is just learning to walk. How hard is it to keep him from falling and hurting himself? Just as you follow close behind that toddler to protect him, God follows close behind you—to protect you.

God Knows You by Name

Quite a thought, isn't it? Your name on God's hand. Your name on God's lips. Maybe you've seen your name in some special places. On an award or diploma. . . . But to think that your name is on God's hand and on God's lips . . . my, could it be?

Or perhaps you have never seen your name honored. And you can't remember when you heard it spoken with kindness. If so, it may be more difficult for you to believe that God knows your name.

But he does. Written on his hand. Spoken by his mouth. Whispered by his lips. Your name.

When God Whispers Your Name

Read Together

"I have written your name on my hand."

ISAIAH 49:16

God Knows Your Name

What a thought! Your name is written on God's hand. Your name is on God's lips. Maybe you've seen your name in some special places. On an award or a trophy. But to think that your name is on God's hand and on God's lips . . . Wow! Could it be?

Or maybe you have never had your name honored. Maybe you've never made the honor roll. Or won the trophy. Or been chosen for the team. If so, it may be even harder for you to believe that God knows your name.

But he does. It's written on his hand. Spoken by his mouth. Whispered by his lips. *Your name.*

GROWING IN GRACE

Close your eyes and picture God gently calling your name. Do you hear him? Do you see your name written in beautiful letters on the palm of his hand? Read Psalm 139 to discover just how well the Lord knows you—and how much he loves you.

A Work in Progress

God is not finished with you yet. Oh, you may think he is. You may think you've peaked. You may think he's got someone else to do the job.

If so, think again.

"God began doing a good work in you, and I am sure he will continue it until it is finished when Jesus Christ comes again" (Philippians 1:6).

Did you see what God is doing? *A good work in you.*

Did you see when he will be finished? *When Jesus comes again.*

May I spell out the message? *God ain't finished with you yet.*

When God Whispers Your Name

Read Together

Jesus will keep you strong until the end so that there will be no wrong in you on the day our Lord Jesus Christ comes again.

1 CORINTHIANS 1:8

A Work in Progress

God is not finished with you yet. Oh, you may think he is. You may think you're right where you need to be. You may think you've got life all figured out.

If so, think again. You've still got a lot of growing to do.

"God began doing a good work in you. And he will continue it until it is finished when Jesus Christ comes again" (Philippians 1:6 ICB).

Did you see what God is doing? *A good work in you.* Did you see when he will be finished? *When Jesus comes again.* Let me make God's message clear for you: *God ain't finished with you yet.*

GROWING IN GRACE

God ain't finished with you yet. But what will you look like— and be like—when he is? Paint your best self-portrait. Just the way you look right now. Then paint another portrait. This time show how you think you'll look when God is finished with you—in heaven.

Play Sublimely

Antonio Stradivari was a seventeenth-century violin maker whose name in its Latin form, *Stradivarius*, has become synonymous with excellence. He once said that to make a violin less than his best would be to rob God, who could not make Antonio Stradivari's violins without Antonio.

He was right. God could not make Stradivarius violins without Antonio Stradivari. Certain gifts were given to that craftsman that no other violin maker possessed.

In the same vein, there are certain things you can do that no one else can. Perhaps it is parenting, or constructing houses, or encouraging the discouraged. There are things that *only* you can do, and you are alive to do them. In the great orchestra we call life, you have an instrument and a song, and you owe it to God to play them both sublimely.

The Applause of Heaven

Read Together

I praise you because you made me in an amazing and wonderful way.

PSALM 139:14

The Best That You Can

Antonio Stradivari was a violin maker in the 1700s. His name in its Latin form, *Stradivarius*, has come to mean "excellence." He once said that to make a violin less than his best would be to rob God, who could not make Antonio Stradivari's violins without Antonio.

He was right. God could not make Stradivarius violins without Antonio Stradivari. Certain gifts were given to that craftsman that no other violin maker possessed.

In the same way, there are certain things you can do that no one else can. Perhaps it is encouraging your friends, playing basketball, or drawing the beauty of God's creation. There are things that only *you* can do, and you were put here by God to do them. Pretend that life is a great orchestra and you have been given an instrument and a song. You owe it to God to play them both the very best that you can.

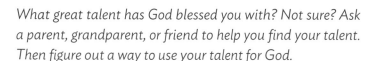

GROWING IN GRACE

What great talent has God blessed you with? Not sure? Ask a parent, grandparent, or friend to help you find your talent. Then figure out a way to use your talent for God.

The Branch and the Vine

God wants to be as close to us as a branch is to a vine. One is an extension of the other. It's impossible to tell where one starts and the other ends. The branch isn't connected only at the moment of bearing fruit. The gardener doesn't keep the branches in a box and then, on the day he wants grapes, glue them to the vine. No, the branch constantly draws nutrition from the vine. . . .

God also uses the temple to depict the intimacy he desires. "Don't you know," Paul writes, "that your body is the temple of the Holy Spirit, who lives in you and was given to you by God?" (1 Corinthians 6:19 TEV). Think with me about the temple for a moment. . . . God didn't come and go, appear and disappear. He was a permanent presence, always available.

What incredibly good news for us! We are NEVER away from God!

Just Like Jesus

Read Together

"Remain in me, and I will remain in you. A branch cannot produce fruit alone but must remain in the vine."

JOHN 15:4

The Branch and the Vine

A branch is connected to a vine. One is a part of the other. It's impossible to tell where the branch starts and the vine ends.

The branch isn't connected to the vine only when it bears fruit. The gardener doesn't keep the branches in a box and then—on the day he wants grapes—run out and glue the branches to the vine. No, the branch lives on the vine and gets its strength from the vine.

That's the kind of relationship God wants with you. God doesn't want you to turn to him only when you need something or when something is wrong. God wants your thoughts and your heart to be with him always.

If a branch is cut off the vine, it begins to dry up. It has lost the source of its life. In the same way, when you are cut off from God, your heart begins to dry up. You have lost the source of your life.

Stay connected to the vine—to God—and he will keep you strong.

GROWING IN GRACE

With your parents' permission, cut a small branch from a tree. Place it where you will see it every day. What happens after a few hours? A few days? Now imagine you are the branch and God is the tree. If you cut yourself off from him, how will you change?

God's Mighty Hand

With one decision, history began. Existence became measurable.

Out of nothing came light.

Out of light came day.

Then came sky . . . and earth.

And on this earth? A mighty hand went to work.

Canyons were carved. Oceans were dug. Mountains erupted out of flatlands. Stars were flung. A universe sparkled.

Look to the canyons to see the Creator's splendor. Touch the flowers and see his delicacy. Listen to the thunder and hear his power. . . .

Today you will encounter God's creation. When you see the beauty around you, let each detail remind you to lift your head in praise. Express your appreciation for God's creation. Encourage others to see the beauty of his creation.

In the Eye of the Storm

Read Together

Through his power all things were made—things in heaven and on earth, things seen and unseen.

COLOSSIANS 1:16

God's Mighty Hand

"Let there be . . ."

With those three words, history began. Time began. "Let there be . . ." light. And "let there be . . ." day and night, sky and earth. And then on this earth the mighty hand of God went to work.

He carved out the canyons and dug the deepest oceans. He made mountains burst out of the flatlands. He flung the stars into the sky and made the universe sparkle with his light.

Do you want to see God's might? Look at the mountains. Want to see his gentleness? Touch his wildflowers. Want to hear his power? Listen to the thunder.

Today you will come face-to-face with God's creation. When you see the beauty of nature all around you, let it remind you to give thanks to God for the world he made.

GROWING IN GRACE

Any time of year has its own beauty, and we can really enjoy nature. Go outside. Take a walk. Pick a flower. Feel the breeze. Praise God for the creative work of his mighty hand.

Set Apart

John the Baptist would never get hired today. No church would touch him. He was a public relations disaster. He "wore clothes made from camel's hair, had a leather belt around his waist, and ate locusts and wild honey" (Mark 1:6). Who would want to look at a guy like that every Sunday?

His message was as rough as his dress: a no-nonsense, bare-fisted challenge to repent because God was on his way.

John the Baptist set himself apart for one task, to be a voice of Christ. Everything about John centered on his purpose. His dress. His diet. His actions. His demands.

You don't have to be like the world to have an impact on the world. You don't have to be like the crowd to change the crowd. You don't have to lower yourself down to their level to lift them up to your level. Holiness doesn't seek to be odd. Holiness seeks to be like God.

A Gentle Thunder

Read Together

Anyone who wants to be a friend of the world becomes God's enemy.

JAMES 4:4

John the Baptist

John the Baptist would never get hired as a preacher today. What would the people think? Can't you just hear them whispering? "His clothes are 'made from camel's hair' (Mark 1:6)! Did you see him? He 'ate locusts and wild honey' (Mark 1:6)! I'm not sitting next to him in Sunday school!"

John's message was as no-nonsense as his dress: confess your sins and turn away from them because the Lord is on his way (Matthew 3:2). John the Baptist set himself apart from the rest for one reason—to tell others about Jesus. Everything about John focused on that one task. His dress. His food. His words. His actions.

You don't have to be like the world to make a difference in the world. You don't have to be like the crowd to change the crowd. You don't have to lower yourself down to their level to lift them up to God's level.

Holiness doesn't try to fit in. Holiness tries to be like God.

GROWING IN GRACE

Take a good look at yourself. What kinds of things are you doing just to fit in with the crowd? What are you wearing or watching? Is it worth it? Are these things pleasing to God? Or are there some things you need to change?

God Honors Our Choice

How could a loving God send people to hell? That's a commonly asked question. The question itself reveals a couple of misconceptions.

First, God does not *send* people to hell. He simply honors their choice. Hell is the ultimate expression of God's high regard for the dignity of man. He has never forced us to choose him, even when that means we would choose hell. . . .

No, God does not "send" people to hell. Nor does he send *people* to hell. That is the second misconception.

The word "people" is neutral, implying innocence. Nowhere does Scripture teach that innocent people are condemned. People do not go to hell. Sinners do. The rebellious do. The self-centered do. So how could a loving God send people to hell? He doesn't. He simply honors the choice of sinners.

When Christ Comes

Read Together

We all have wandered away like sheep;
each of us has gone his own way.

Isaiah 53:6

God Lets Us Choose

How could a loving God punish people for all eternity? People often ask that question. But we need to get a couple of things straight.

First, *God* does not choose to punish people. God tells us what will happen if we do not obey his Word, and then he lets *us* choose. If we choose not to follow his Word, then we choose to be punished. But if we choose to obey his Word, then he rewards us with heaven. The choice is ours. God simply respects our choice.

Second, God does not punish *people*. God punishes sinners. He punishes those who have chosen to do wrong and disobey him.

And, last, no one *has* to be punished. God offers a way for everyone to get to heaven. All we have to do is believe in his Son and obey his Word. But God won't force us to believe—it has to be our choice.

GROWING IN GRACE

Waiting until you have to choose makes it harder to make the right decision. So decide now. What will you do if a friend offers you drugs or alcohol? What if you're tempted to lie? Will you cheat to get what you want? Deciding today makes choosing a lot easier tomorrow.

Walking with God

Healthy marriages have a sense of "remaining." The husband remains in the wife, and she remains in him. There is a tenderness, an honesty, an ongoing communication. The same is true in our relationship with God. Sometimes we go to him with our joys, and sometimes we go with our hurts, but we always go. And as we go, the more we go, the more we become like him. Paul says we are being changed from "glory to glory" (2 Corinthians 3:18 KJV).

People who live long lives together eventually begin to sound alike, to talk alike, even to think alike. As we walk with God, we take on his thoughts, his principles, his attitudes. We take on his heart.

Just Like Jesus

Read Together

You were taught to be made new in your hearts, to become a new person. . . . Made to be like God—made to be truly good and holy.

EPHESIANS 4:23–24

Walking with God

Healthy families love each other. They are kind and tender with each other, and they are honest with each other. As we spend time with our families, we become like them. God designed our homes to be the place where we can always go to find love.

The same is true in our relationship with God. Sometimes we go to him with our joys, and sometimes we go with our hurts. But we always go, and we always find his love. And the more we go, the more we become like him. Paul said, "This change in us brings more and more glory" (2 Corinthians 3:18 ICB).

People who live long lives together begin to sound alike, to talk alike, even to think alike. As we grow closer to God, we begin to sound like him and think more like him. And hopefully our hearts begin to look more like his every day.

GROWING IN GRACE

Look at your grandparents or another older couple who've been married a long time. Ask if you can see some photos of them through the years. Have they started to look alike? Are there habits that they both have? Do they even finish each other's sentences?

Dealing with the Past

Anger. It's easy to define: the noise of the soul. *Anger.* The unseen irritant of the heart. *Anger.* The relentless invader of silence. . . .

The louder it gets the more desperate we become. . . .

Some of you are thinking . . . *you don't have any idea how hard my life has been.* And you're right, I don't. But I have a very clear idea how miserable your future will be unless you deal with your anger.

X-ray the world of the vengeful and behold the tumor of bitterness: black, menacing, malignant. Carcinoma of the spirit. Its fatal fibers creep around the edge of the heart and ravage it. Yesterday you can't alter, but your reaction to yesterday you can. The past you cannot change, but your response to your past you can.

When God Whispers Your Name

Read Together

Don't get angry.
    Don't be upset; it only leads to trouble.

PSALM 37:8

Dealing with Anger

Anger. It's loud. It's loud in your heart. It's loud in your mind. And it can be just plain loud.

The louder it gets, the more desperate we become.

Some of you are thinking, *You don't have any idea how hard my life is. Homework. Tryouts. Bullies. Fighting parents.* You're right. I don't know how tough your life is right now. But I have a very clear idea of how miserable your future will be if you don't deal with your anger.

Anger is like a dark thundercloud: black, threatening, and terrible. It's like a storm in your heart that is threatening to turn into a tornado. You can't change what other people do, but you can change how you act toward them. You can't always help being angry, but you can control what you do with your anger. Ask God to help you—because he will.

GROWING IN GRACE

There will always be things—and people—that make you angry. Like the bully who always picks on you, piles of homework, or being laughed at. Being angry is okay, but sinning is not. Avoid sin by deciding now what you will do the next time something makes you angry.

Who Is My Brother?

Seems to me God gives a lot more grace than we'd ever imagine.

We could do the same.

I'm not for watering down the truth or compromising the gospel. But if a fellow with a pure heart calls God *Father*, can't I call that same man *Brother*? If God doesn't make doctrinal perfection a requirement for family membership, should I?

And if we never agree, can't we agree to disagree? If God can tolerate my mistakes, can't I tolerate the mistakes of others? . . . If God allows me with my foibles and failures to call him *Father*, shouldn't I extend the same grace to others?

When God Whispers Your Name

Read Together

"Lord, how many times shall I forgive my brother or sister who sins against me? Up to seven times?" Jesus answered, ". . . seventy-seven times."

MATTHEW 18:21–22 NIV

Give a Little Grace

Seems to me that God gives us a lot more grace than we could ever imagine.

Seems to me that we could do the same for others.

You know that you're not perfect. And, thankfully, God doesn't ask you to be. That's what his grace is for—it washes away all those times that you're not perfect.

When God gives you his grace, he then asks you to do something for him: *remember that no one else is perfect either*. Give a little grace to those around you.

Because it's going to happen. Your brother or sister will say something mean. Your best friend will hurt your feelings. Once in a while even your mom or dad might snap at you. When those things happen, don't hold a grudge. Forgive them, and give a little grace—because God has given you a whole lot.

GROWING IN GRACE

God asks you to give others the same grace that he gives you, but he also wants you to give grace to yourself. You're not perfect, and you will mess up. Someday you will do that thing you said you wouldn't do. And when you do, ask God to forgive you. Just don't forget to forgive yourself too.

Peace Treaties of Love

Jesus described for his followers what he came to do. He came to build a relationship with people. He came to take away enmity, to take away the strife, to take away the isolation that existed between God and man. Once he bridged that, once he overcame that, he said, "I will call you friends."

In repairing a relationship, it's essential to realize that no friendship is perfect, no marriage is perfect, no person is perfect. With the resolve that you are going to make a relationship work, you can develop peace treaties of love and tolerance and harmony to transform a difficult situation into something beautiful.

Walking with the Savior

Read Together

Be sure that no one pays back wrong for wrong, but always try to do what is good for each other and for all people.

1 THESSALONIANS 5:15

Decide to Love

It's important to know that no friendship is perfect, no family is perfect, no person is perfect. And you're not perfect. So when you decide to make a relationship work—to get along—you have to remember that people will still make mistakes, will still get on your nerves sometimes, will still hurt your feelings.

So how do you get along with others? Look at what God says in Romans 12:10–18 (ICB): "Give your brothers and sisters more honor than you want for yourselves. . . . Wish good for those who do bad things to you. . . . Be happy with those who are happy. Be sad with those who are sad. . . . If someone does wrong to you, do not pay him back by doing wrong to him. . . . Do your best to live in peace with everyone."

In other words . . . *choose to love.*

GROWING IN GRACE

Agape love is "anyway love." It is a choice, not just a warm, fuzzy feeling. It's the kind of love that says, I'll do what's best for you even when you hurt my feelings, or trick me, or laugh at me. I'll treat you the way I wish you would treat me.

Forgiveness Frees the Soul

Is there any emotion that imprisons the soul more than the unwilling-ness to forgive? What do you do when people mistreat you or those you love? Does the fire of anger boil within you, with leaping flames consuming your emotions? Or do you reach somewhere, to some source of cool water and pull out a bucket of mercy—to free yourself?

Don't get on the roller coaster of resentment and anger. You be the one who says, "Yes, he mistreated me, but I am going to be like Christ. I'll be the one who says, 'Forgive them, Father, they don't know what they're doing.'"

Walking with the Savior

Read Together

If you suffer for doing good, and you are patient, then God is pleased.

1 PETER 2:20

Put Out the Fire

What do you do when people mistreat you or those you love? Do you feel anger bubble inside you? Do flames of hate burn your heart? Does your face burn red and hot?

Or do you reach up to Jesus? Do you ask him to help you control the angry fire? Do you pull out a bucket of mercy—and throw it on the angry flames? Do you put out the fire?

Don't get on the roller coaster of anger. Be the one who says, "Yes, he treated me wrong, but I am going to be like Christ. I'll be the one who says, 'Father, forgive them. They don't know what they are doing'" (Luke 23:34 ICB).

If Jesus could look down from the cross and say those words, then so can you. Ask him to help you put out the fire.

GROWING IN GRACE

The next time you feel like you can't forgive someone, picture Jesus on the cross. He didn't die there so that you could hold a grudge. Pray for his help to forgive those who have done you wrong.

Your Whispering Thoughts

Imagine considering every moment as a potential time of communion with God. By the time your life is over, you will have spent six months at stoplights, eight months opening junk mail, a year and a half looking for lost stuff (double that number in my case), and a whopping five years standing in various lines.

Why don't you give these moments to God? By giving God your whispering thoughts, the common becomes uncommon. Simple phrases such as "Thank you, Father," "Be sovereign in this hour, O Lord," "You are my resting place, Jesus" can turn a commute into a pilgrimage. You needn't leave your office or kneel in your kitchen. Just pray where you are. Let the kitchen become a cathedral or the classroom a chapel. Give God your whispering thoughts.

Just Like Jesus

Read Together

God, examine me and know my heart;
test me and know my anxious thoughts.

PSALM 139:23

Your Whispering Thoughts

Imagine—what if you thought of every second of every day as a chance to talk to God?

By the time your life is over, you will have spent six months waiting at stoplights, a year and a half looking for lost stuff, and a whopping five years standing in lines.

Why don't you give these "lost" moments to God? By giving God your thoughts during these moments, the ordinary becomes extraordinary. Your prayers don't need to be out loud. Your eyes don't have to be closed. Prayers can simply be silent whispers— just between you and God.

Simple prayers—such as "Thank you, Father," "Be with me this day, God," and "I trust you, Jesus"—can turn a car ride into worship. You don't need a special place. Just pray where you are. Let the kitchen become a church and the classroom become a chapel. Give God your whispering thoughts.

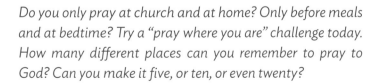

GROWING IN GRACE

Do you only pray at church and at home? Only before meals and at bedtime? Try a "pray where you are" challenge today. How many different places can you remember to pray to God? Can you make it five, or ten, or even twenty?

Closer Than You Think

When the disciples saw Jesus in the middle of their stormy night, they called him a ghost. A phantom. . . . To them, the glow was anything but God.

When we see gentle lights on the horizon, we often have the same reaction. We dismiss occasional kindness as apparitions, accidents, or anomalies. Anything but God. . . .

And because we look for the bonfire, we miss the candle. Because we listen for the shout, we miss the whisper.

But it is in burnished candles that God comes, and through whispered promises he speaks: "When you doubt, look around; I am closer than you think."

In the Eye of the Storm

Read Together

Jesus spoke to them, saying, "Be of good cheer! It is I; do not be afraid."

MATTHEW 14:27 NKJV

Closer Than You Think

The storm at sea was terrible. The wind howled. The waves beat against the boat. And the disciples battled for their lives. They were already frightened. So when they saw Jesus walking toward them on the water, they called him a ghost. A phantom. To them, the glow was anything but God.

When we see gentle lights in the middle of the stormy parts of life, we often think the same thing. We see the kindness, the helping hand, the answer. But we think they are just an accident, a chance happening, or good luck. We think they are anything but God.

But God doesn't burst into the room with ten thousand angels to help you. When you're in the middle of a bad day or a bad problem, he uses the people around you to help. That friendly hug, that offer to help, that unexpected answer just when you needed it—they aren't accidents. They are God. He is closer than you think.

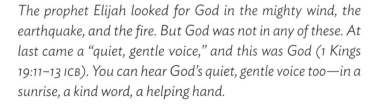

GROWING IN GRACE

The prophet Elijah looked for God in the mighty wind, the earthquake, and the fire. But God was not in any of these. At last came a "quiet, gentle voice," and this was God (1 Kings 19:11–13 ICB). You can hear God's quiet, gentle voice too—in a sunrise, a kind word, a helping hand.

The Purpose of Life

Mine deep enough in every heart and you'll find it: a longing for meaning, a quest for purpose. As surely as a child breathes, he will someday wonder, "What is the purpose of my life?"

Some search for meaning in a career. "My purpose is to be a dentist." Fine vocation but hardly a justification for existence. They opt to be a human "doing" rather than a human "being." Who they are is what they do; consequently they do a lot. They work many hours because if they don't work, they don't have an identity.

For others, who they are is what they have. They find meaning in a new car or a new house or new clothes. These people are great for the economy and rough on the budget because they are always seeking meaning in something they own. . . . Some try sports, entertainment, cults, sex, you name it.

All mirages in the desert of purpose. . . .

Shouldn't we face the truth? If we don't acknowledge God, we are flotsam in the universe.

In the Grip of Grace

Read Together

"Love the Lord your God with all your heart, all your soul, and all your mind."

MATTHEW 22:37

110

Why Am I Here?

Dig deep enough in every heart and you'll find it: the wish to understand why God created you. As surely as you breathe, you will someday wonder, "Why am I here? Why did God make me?"

Some people search for the answer in their work. These people believe that who they are is what they *do*, so they do a lot. "I am here to be an A+ student." That's a great goal, but not exactly a reason for living.

For other people, who they are is what they *have*. They find meaning in the right clothes, right house, right toys. They believe their reason for being here is tied to the things they own. Others try to have all the fun they possibly can, and still others try to be the sports star or the movie star.

But none of these things are the right answer to the question "Why am I here?" We only have one purpose in life. One reason for being here. To praise God.

So shouldn't we do just that?

GROWING IN GRACE

How do you want people to describe you? As cool, or as committed to Christ? Write down words you think describe Jesus, like patient, kind, loving, selfless. Now try to live so that people will say those same things about you. That's the kind of life that will praise God.

Repentance Is a Decision

No one is happier than the one who has sincerely repented of wrong. Repentance is the decision to turn from selfish desires and seek God. It is a genuine, sincere regret that creates sorrow and moves us to admit wrong and desire to do better.

It's an inward conviction that expresses itself in outward actions.

You look at the love of God and you can't believe he's loved you like he has, and this realization motivates you to change your life. That is the nature of repentance.

Walking with the Savior

Read Together

Perhaps you do not understand that God is kind to you so you will change your hearts and lives.

ROMANS 2:4

Spiritual U-Turns

Have you ever heard the word *repent*? Christians use that word a lot, but what does it really mean? *Repent* means more than just saying we're sorry. *Repent* means we stop doing what is wrong and we try to do what is right. It is turning away from selfishness and sin and turning to God. It's like a spiritual U-turn.

When we repent, the sadness we feel on the *inside* shows itself in the way we act on the *outside*.

You look at the love of God and compare it to your sins. You can't believe he loves you like he does—with all your mess-ups and mix-ups. And knowing this makes you want to change the way you live. That is what it means to repent.

GROWING IN GRACE

Have you ever been in the car with your parents when they realized they were going the wrong way? Do they just keep going? No, they stop. But they don't just stop. They turn around and start going the right way. That's repentance—not just stopping, but turning around and going the right way.

More Than Meets the Eye

Faith is trusting what the eye can't see.

>Eyes see the prowling lion. Faith sees Daniel's angel.

>Eyes see storms. Faith sees Noah's rainbow.

>Eyes see giants. Faith sees Canaan.

>Your eyes see your faults. Your faith sees your Savior.

>Your eyes see your guilt. Your faith sees his blood.

>Your eyes look in the mirror and see a sinner, a failure, a promise-breaker. But by faith you look in the mirror and see a robed prodigal bearing the ring of grace on your finger and the kiss of your Father on your face.

When God Whispers Your Name

Read Together

Faith means being sure of the things we hope for and knowing that something is real even if we do not see it.

HEBREWS 11:1

Believing in What You Don't See

Faith is trusting what our eyes can't see.

- Human eyes see the prowling lions. Daniel's faith sees the angel close the lions' mouths.
- Human eyes see storms. Noah's faith sees the rainbow.
- Human eyes see a giant. David's faith sees the giant Goliath fall.
- Your eyes see your faults. Your faith sees Jesus your Savior.

When you look in the mirror, do you see your mistakes, your sins? It's easy for our human eyes to only see what is wrong. We need to use our "eyes of faith"—the way God sees things—to see what is right. Look in the mirror again, using your eyes of faith. I can tell you what God sees there—his beloved child, the one he has promised all of heaven to.

GROWING IN GRACE

We trust our eyes to show us what is real and what is not. But our eyes can't see everything. What are some real but invisible things? Wind. Love. Kindness. Electricity. Can you think of others? You may not be able to see them, but you can see what they do—just like you can see what God does.

God Is in Your Corner

When I was seven years old, I ran away from home. I'd had enough of my father's rules and decided I could make it on my own, thank you very much. With my clothes in a paper bag, I stormed out the back gate and marched down the alley. But I didn't go far. I got to the end of the alley and remembered I was hungry, so I went back home.

Though the rebellion was brief, it was rebellion nonetheless. And had you stopped me on that prodigal path . . . I just might have told you how I felt. I just might have said, "I don't need a father. I'm too big for the rules of my family."

I didn't hear the rooster crow like Peter did. I didn't feel the fish belch like Jonah did. I didn't get a robe and a ring and sandals like the prodigal did. But I learned from my father on earth what those three learned from their Father in heaven. Our God is no fair-weather Father. He's not into this love-'em-and-leave-'em stuff. I can count on him to be in my corner no matter how I perform. You can, too.

The Great House of God

Read Together

The LORD himself will go before you. He will be with you; he will not leave you or forget you.

DEUTERONOMY 31:8

God Is on Your Side

When I was seven years old, I ran away from home. I'd had enough of my father's rules. With my clothes in a paper bag, I stormed out the back gate and marched down the alley. But I didn't go far. I got to the end of the alley and realized I was hungry, so I went back home.

Although my disobedience was brief, it was still disobedience. And if you had stopped me in that alley, I just might have told you how I felt: "I don't need a father. I'm too big for his rules."

I didn't hear the rooster crow like Peter did. Or the fish belch like Jonah did. I didn't get a robe like the prodigal son did. But I learned from my earthly father what they learned from their heavenly Father: I can count on God to be on my side no matter what I do. You can too.

GROWING IN GRACE

Every family has its own rules. Be kind. Wipe your feet. Respect everyone. Wash your hands. Say please and thank you. God's family has its rules too. Just two of them. Find out what they are in Luke 10:27.

We Shall See Him

What will happen when you see Jesus?

You will see unblemished purity and unbending strength. You will feel his unending presence and know his unbridled protection. And—all that he is, you will be, for you will be like Jesus. Wasn't that the promise of John? "We know that when Christ comes again, we will be like him, because we will see him as he really is" (1 John 3:2).

Since you'll be pure as snow, you will never sin again; . . . you will never stumble again; . . . you will never feel lonely again; . . . you will never doubt again.

When Christ comes, you will dwell in the light of God. And you will see him as he really is.

When Christ Comes

Read Together

Now we see a dim reflection, as if we were looking into a mirror, but then we shall see clearly.

1 CORINTHIANS 13:12

Seeing Jesus Clearly

What will it be like to finally see Jesus face-to-face? How will it feel?

I believe it will be greater than anything we could ever imagine. But I like to imagine anyway. And I imagine it will be better than Christmas morning, better than a birthday, better than an ice-cream sundae—all rolled into one!

When we see Jesus face-to-face, we will be looking into the eyes of One who loves us more than anyone else ever could. And his love will fill us with complete joy and peace.

All our sins and mistakes will be completely washed away forever. There will be no more guilt or shame, no more loneliness or being left out. We will never mess up again or stumble again or doubt again. Why? Because "when Christ comes again, we will be like him" (1 John 3:2 ICB).

And I can't wait!

GROWING IN GRACE

First Corinthians 13:12 (ICB) says, "Now we see as if we are looking into a dark mirror. But [then] . . . we shall see clearly." Take a mirror into a dark room. A little hard to see your reflection, isn't it? Now turn on the light. Much clearer! That's what heaven will be like—we'll be able to see Jesus clearly.

If Only . . .

Maybe your past isn't much to brag about. Maybe you've seen raw evil. And now you . . . have to make a choice. Do you rise above the past and make a difference? Or do you remain controlled by the past and make excuses? . . .

Many choose the convalescent homes of the heart. Healthy bodies. Sharp minds. But retired dreams. Back and forth they rock in the chair of regret, repeating the terms of surrender. Lean closely and you will hear them: "If only."

"If only I'd been born somewhere else . . ."

"If only I'd been treated fairly . . ."

Maybe you've used those words. Maybe you have every right to use them. . . . If such is the case . . . go to John's gospel and read Jesus' words: "Human life comes from human parents, but spiritual life comes from the Spirit" (John 3:6).

When God Whispers Your Name

Read Together

So now you are not a slave; you are God's child, and God will give you the blessing he promised, because you are his child.

Galatians 4:7

If Only . . .

It's easy to look at the world around you and say, "If only . . . If only I could make the team . . . If only I could be popular . . . If only I had the right clothes or the right friends . . . If only we had more money . . . If only my family were different . . ."

Your list could go on and on and on.

I believe God has an "if only" list too. His list probably goes something like this: "If only he knew how much I love him . . . If only she would ask for my help . . . If only he would trust me . . . If only she would let me save her . . ."

There are a lot of "if only" things that you can't do anything about. But you can choose to do something about God's "if only" list. You can choose to believe in him and to obey his Word—and you can make God's "if onlys" come true.

GROWING IN GRACE

You decide what kind of person you will be. Whether you were blessed with a great family or a not-so-great one, you get to decide if you want to be like them. But God is most interested in how much you want to be like him. It's your choice.

You Have Captured God's Heart

Have you ever noticed the way a groom looks at his bride during the wedding? I have. Perhaps it's my vantage point. As the minister of the wedding, I'm positioned next to the groom. . . .

If the light is just so and the angle just right, I can see a tiny reflection in his eyes. Her reflection. And the sight of her reminds him why he is here. His jaw relaxes and his forced smile softens. He forgets he's wearing a tux. He forgets his sweat-soaked shirt. . . . When he sees her, any thought of escape becomes a joke again. For it's written all over his face, "Who could bear to live without this bride?"

And such are precisely the feelings of Jesus. Look long enough into the eyes of our Savior and, there, too, you will see a bride. Dressed in fine linen. Clothed in pure grace. . . . She is the bride . . . walking toward him. . . .

And who is this bride for whom Jesus longs? . . . You are. You have captured the heart of God.

When Christ Comes

Read Together

As a man rejoices over his new wife,
　　so your God will rejoice over you.

ISAIAH 62:5

The Joy of God's Heart

Have you ever seen the way a groom looks at his bride during the wedding? I have. Perhaps it's because of where I'm standing. As the minister at the wedding, I'm standing right next to the groom.

If the light is just right, I can see a tiny reflection in his eyes. Her reflection. And the sight of her reminds him why he is here. His jaw softens, and his smile becomes real again. He forgets he's wearing a tux. He forgets his sweat-soaked shirt. When he sees her, any thought of running away becomes a joke. For it's written all over his face, "I can't live without my bride!"

And those are the exact same feelings Jesus has. Look long enough into his eyes, and you will see the reflection of someone. Dressed in white. Clothed in pure grace.

And who is this person Jesus is waiting for? *It's you!* You are the joy of God's heart.

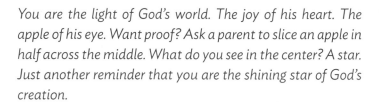

GROWING IN GRACE

You are the light of God's world. The joy of his heart. The apple of his eye. Want proof? Ask a parent to slice an apple in half across the middle. What do you see in the center? A star. Just another reminder that you are the shining star of God's creation.

God's Plans

When we submit to God's plans, we can trust our desires. Our assignment is found at the intersection of God's plan and our pleasures. *What do you love to do? What brings you joy? What gives you a sense of satisfaction?*

Some long to feed the poor. Others enjoy leading the church. . . . Each of us has been made to serve God in a unique way. . . .

The longings of your heart, then, are not incidental; they are critical messages. The desires of your heart are not to be ignored; they are to be consulted. As the wind turns the weather vane, so God uses your passions to turn your life. God is too gracious to ask you to do something you hate.

Just Like Jesus

Read Together

Enjoy serving the LORD,
  and he will give you what you want.

PSALM 37:4

God's Plan for Your Life

When we choose to follow God's plans, we can trust our wants and desires. Our life's mission—our purpose—is found at the place where God's plan and our pleasures meet. *What do you love to do? What makes you happy? What gives you a sense of satisfaction?* God will use those things in his plan for your life.

Some people feel a need to help the poor. Others enjoy leading others at church. Each of us has been made to serve God in our own special way.

The things you enjoy doing are no accidents. They are important messages. The things you love to do shouldn't be ignored; they should be respected. Just as the wind turns the direction of the weather vane, so God uses the things you love to do to turn the direction of your life. God is too kind to ask you to do something you hate.

GROWING IN GRACE

As you search for your life's mission, ask yourself these questions: What do you love to do? What is your favorite part of church? What makes you smile the most? Now find people in your church who have those same interests and ask them how they use their interests to serve God.

The True Son of God

Read this verse: "Then those who were in the boat worshiped him, saying, 'Truly you are the Son of God'" (Matthew 14:33 NIV).

After the storm, [the disciples] worshiped him. They had never, as a group, done that before. Never. Check it out. Open your Bible. Search for a time when the disciples corporately praised him.

You won't find it.

You won't find them worshiping when he heals the leper. Forgives the adulteress. Preaches to the masses. They were willing to follow. Willing to leave family. Willing to cast out demons. Willing to be in the army.

But only after the incident on the sea did they worship him. Why? Simple. This time they were the ones who were saved.

In the Eye of the Storm

Read Together

His followers went to him and woke him, saying, "Lord, save us! We will drown!" Jesus answered, "Why are you afraid?"

MATTHEW 8:25–26

He Saves Us

The Bible says that after Jesus calmed the storm, "those who were in the boat worshiped Jesus and said, 'Truly you are the Son of God!'" (Matthew 14:33 ICB).

After the storm, the disciples worshiped him. As far as we know, they had never, as a group, done that before. Never. Check it out. Open your Bible. Search for a time when the disciples all joined together and praised Jesus. You won't find it.

You won't find them worshiping when he healed the leper. Reached out to the woman at the well. Preached to the masses. They were willing to follow. Willing to leave family. Willing to cast out demons. Willing to be in the Lord's army.

But only after Jesus stilled the storm on the sea did they worship him. Why?

Simple. This time they knew *they* were the ones who had been saved.

GROWING IN GRACE

God's saving love isn't just for people in general. It is for you— you personally. Don't believe it? Check out Isaiah 43:1 (ICB): "I have saved you. I have called you by name, and you are mine." God is calling your name—so answer him.

A Parent's Precious Prayers

Never underestimate the ponderings of a Christian parent. Never underestimate the power that comes when a parent pleads with God on behalf of a child. Who knows how many prayers are being answered right now because of the faithful ponderings of a parent ten or twenty years ago? God listens to thoughtful parents.

Praying for our children is a noble task. If what we are doing, in this fast-paced society, is taking us away from prayer time for our children, we're doing too much. There is nothing more special, more precious than time that a parent spends struggling and pondering with God on behalf of a child.

Walking with the Savior

Read Together

"All your children will be taught by the LORD,
and they will have much peace."

ISAIAH 54:13

Prayers for Parents

Pay attention to the prayers of a Christian parent. Pay attention to the power that comes when a parent asks God to be with or help a child. Who knows what prayers will be answered in your life ten or twenty years from now because of your parents' faithful prayers right now? God listens to thoughtful parents.

And God listens to thoughtful children. Just as your parents pray for you, take time to pray for your parents. They are God's children too. They need his help, his guidance, his wisdom just as much as you do. There is nothing more special, more precious than the time that a child spends struggling with prayers to God. Your prayers are heard—and answered—in heaven.

GROWING IN GRACE

It doesn't matter how old you are, there are few things more wonderful than hearing your name lifted up in prayer. Ask your parents if you can pray together. Listen as they pray for you—and let them hear your prayers for them.

The Temple of God's Spirit

You will live forever in this body. It will be different, mind you. What is now crooked will be straightened. What is now faulty will be fixed. Your body will be different, but you won't have a different body. You will have this one. Does that change the view you have of it? I hope so.

God has a high regard for your body. You should as well. Respect it. I did not say worship it. But I did say respect it. It is after all the temple of God. Be careful how you feed it, use it, and maintain it. You wouldn't want anyone trashing your home; God doesn't want anyone trashing his. After all, it is his, isn't it?

When Christ Comes

Read Together

You should know that your body is a temple for the Holy Spirit who is in you. You have received the Holy Spirit from God. So you do not belong to yourselves.

1 CORINTHIANS 6:19

God's Temple

You will live forever in your body—or at least in a perfect version of your body. What is now crooked will be straightened. What is now broken will be fixed. Your body will be different, but you won't have a different body. You will have this one. It will be made new and perfect, but it will be the same one. Does that change the view you have of your body? I hope so.

God created your body, and he loves his creation. You should as well. Respect your body. I did not say worship it, but I did say respect it. After all, the Bible tells us that the human body is the temple of God—the place where the Holy Spirit of God lives. Be careful how you feed it, use it, and take care of it. You wouldn't want anyone trashing your home, would you? Well, God doesn't want anyone trashing his either. After all, it is *his* temple, isn't it?

GROWING IN GRACE

All those things your mom tells you to do—like brush your teeth, eat your veggies, go outside and play—are really about keeping you healthy. Try to add one healthy habit this week. Turn off the TV and shoot some hoops. Choose fruit for your after-school snack. Take care of God's temple.

Four Habits Worth Having

Growth is the goal of the Christian. Maturity is mandatory. If a child ceased to develop, the parent would be concerned, right? . . .

When a Christian stops growing, help is needed. If you are the same Christian you were a few months ago, be careful. You might be wise to get a checkup. Not on your body, but on your heart. Not a physical, but a spiritual.

May I suggest one? . . .

Why don't you check your habits? . . . Make these four habits regular activities and see what happens.

First, the habit of prayer. . . . Second, the habit of study. . . . Third, the habit of giving. . . . And last of all, the habit of fellowship.

When God Whispers Your Name

Read Together

But grow in the grace and knowledge of our Lord and Savior Jesus Christ.

2 PETER 3:18 NIV

Four Habits Worth Having

Growing a stronger faith should be the goal of every Christian. Maturing is a must.

If you stopped growing taller, your parents would be worried, right? They would try to get help for you.

When a Christian's faith stops growing, help is needed too. If you are the same Christian you were last year, be careful. You might need to get a checkup. Not on your body, but on your heart. Not a physical, but a spiritual.

May I suggest one?

Why don't you check your habits? Make these four habits part of your daily activities, and see what happens.

First, the habit of prayer. Second, the habit of Bible study. Third, the habit of giving both your time and your money to God's work here on earth. And, last, the habit of fellowship and friendship with other Christians.

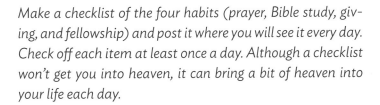

GROWING IN GRACE

Make a checklist of the four habits (prayer, Bible study, giving, and fellowship) and post it where you will see it every day. Check off each item at least once a day. Although a checklist won't get you into heaven, it can bring a bit of heaven into your life each day.

God Is on Our Team

As youngsters, we neighborhood kids would play street football. The minute we got home from school we'd drop the books and hit the pavement. The kid across the street had a dad with a great arm and a strong addiction to football. As soon as he'd pull in the driveway from work we'd start yelling for him to come and play ball. He couldn't resist. Out of fairness he'd always ask, "Which team is losing?" Then he would join that team, which often seemed to be mine.

His appearance in the huddle changed the whole ball game. He was confident, strong, and most of all, he had a plan. We'd circle around him, and he'd look at us and say, "OK boys, here is what we are going to do." The other side was groaning before we left the huddle. You see, we not only had a new plan, we had a new leader.

He brought new life to our team. God does precisely the same. We didn't need a new play; we needed a new plan. We didn't need to trade positions; we needed a new player. That player is Jesus Christ, God's firstborn Son.

In the Grip of Grace

Read Together

When I was helpless, he saved me.

PSALM 116:6

134

A New Leader

When I was growing up, all of us kids in the neighborhood would play street football. The minute we got home from school, we'd hit the pavement. One kid had a dad with a great arm and a love for football. As soon as he'd pull in the driveway from work, we'd start yelling for him to come and play ball. He couldn't resist. Out of fairness he'd always ask, "Which team is losing?" Then he would join that team, which often seemed to be mine.

When he joined the huddle, the whole game changed. He was confident, strong, and, most of all, he had a plan. He'd look at us and say, "Okay, boys, here is what we are going to do." The other side was groaning before we left the huddle. You see, we not only had a new plan, but we also had a new leader. He brought new life to our team.

God does the same thing. In this sinful world, we don't need a new play; we need a new plan. We don't need to trade positions; we need a new player. That player is Jesus.

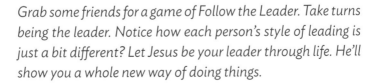

GROWING IN GRACE

Grab some friends for a game of Follow the Leader. Take turns being the leader. Notice how each person's style of leading is just a bit different? Let Jesus be your leader through life. He'll show you a whole new way of doing things.

Changed to His Likeness

What do we know about our resurrected bodies? They will be unlike any we have ever imagined.

Will we look so different that we aren't instantly recognized? Perhaps. (We may need nametags.) Will we be walking through walls? Chances are we'll be doing much more.

Will we still bear the scars from the pain of life? The marks of war. The disfigurements of disease. The wounds of violence. Will these remain on our bodies? That is a very good question. Jesus, at least for forty days, kept his. Will we keep ours? On this issue, we have only opinions, but my opinion is that we won't. Peter tells us that "by his wounds you have been healed" (1 Peter 2:24 NIV). In heaven's accounting, only one wound is worthy to be remembered. And that is the wound of Jesus. Our wounds will be no more.

When Christ Comes

Read Together

By his power to rule all things, he will change our simple bodies and make them like his own glorious body.

PHILIPPIANS 3:21

Our Wounds Are Healed

What do we know about how our bodies will look in heaven? Will we look so different that others won't know who we are? Maybe. (We may need name tags.)

Will we be walking through walls and on water? Chances are we'll be doing much more than that.

Will we still have the scars from this life? The bumps and bruises. The signs of disease. The jagged scars of bike wrecks and broken arms. Will these still be on our bodies? That's a good question. Jesus kept the wounds on his hands, his feet, and his side for at least forty days. Will we keep ours? For this question, we have only opinions, and my opinion is no. Peter told us "we are healed because of his wounds" (1 Peter 2:24 ICB). In heaven, only one wound is worthy of being remembered—the wound of Jesus.

Our wounds and hurts will be healed.

GROWING IN GRACE

Bullying is a terrible sin. It causes wounds that are every bit as serious as wounds to the body. As you go back to school this year, be careful not to hurt those around you. And when you see someone who is hurt by bullying, offer him or her healing words of kindness.

A Life Free of Clutter

The most powerful life is the most simple life. The most powerful life is the life that knows where it's going, that knows where the source of strength is, and the life that stays free of clutter and happenstance and hurriedness.

Being busy is not a sin. Jesus was busy. Paul was busy. Peter was busy. Nothing of significance is achieved without effort and hard work and weariness. Being busy, in and of itself, is not a sin. But being busy in an endless pursuit of *things* that leave us empty and hollow and broken inside—that cannot be pleasing to God.

One source of man's weariness is the pursuit of things that can never satisfy; but which one of us has not been caught up in that pursuit at some time in our life? Our passions, possessions, and pride—these are all *dead* things. When we try to get life out of dead things, the result is only weariness and dissatisfaction.

Walking with the Savior

Read Together

"Your heart will be where your treasure is."

MATTHEW 6:21

Chasing the World

The most powerful life is the most simple life. It's the life that knows God is its source of strength. It's the life that stays free of clutter and busyness.

Being busy is not a sin. Jesus was busy. Paul was busy. Peter was busy. Nothing important happens without hard work and tiredness. No, being busy is not a sin.

But what are we being busy about? Is it an endless chase to get more stuff—the newest, the greatest, the latest? Or an endless search for popularity—be the best, look the best? That kind of busyness will only leave you empty inside. That isn't pleasing to God.

Chasing after the things of this world just makes you tired. Stuff can't make you happy, because there is always more stuff to chase after. Your stuff, your pride, your popularity—these are just things. When you try to make a life out of things instead of God, you only make yourself tired and unhappy.

GROWING IN GRACE

It's okay to have stuff. To want stuff. But it's not okay when stuff is all you think about. Next time you want to buy something, try making yourself wait a week or even two. You may find you don't need that stuff after all.

Don't Panic

Your disappointments too heavy? Read the story of the Emmaus-bound disciples. The Savior they thought was dead now walked beside them. He entered their house and sat at their table. And something happened in their hearts. "It felt like a fire burning in us when Jesus talked to us on the road and explained the Scriptures to us" (Luke 24:32).

Next time you're disappointed, don't panic. Don't give up. Just be patient and let God remind you he's still in control. It ain't over till it's over.

He Still Moves Stones

Read Together

Let us hold firmly to the hope that we have confessed, because we can trust God to do what he promised.

HEBREWS 10:23

Don't Panic

Have you had too many disappointments this week? One too many defeats lately and not nearly enough victories?

Read the story of the disciples on the road to Emmaus in Luke 24:13–35. The Savior they thought was dead was now walking right beside them. He went into their house and sat at their table. And then something happened in their hearts: "When Jesus talked to us on the road, it felt like a fire burning in us. It was exciting when he explained the true meaning of the Scriptures" (Luke 24:32 ICB).

Next time you're disappointed, don't give up. Just be patient and let God remind you that he's still in control. Let him warm your heart with his Word. After all, it ain't over till it's over.

GROWING IN GRACE

Imagine being one of those disciples on the road to Emmaus. What would it be like to lose your Savior and then suddenly find him walking right next to you? Well . . . he is walking right next to you. He's in your house and at your table. And he will explain God's Word to you. He is God's Holy Spirit living in you.

The Wages of Deceit

More than once I've heard people refer to the story [of Ananias and Sapphira] with a nervous chuckle and say, "I'm glad God doesn't still strike people dead for lying." I'm not so sure he doesn't. It seems to me that the wages of deceit is still death. Not death of the body, perhaps, but the death of:

> *a marriage*—Falsehoods are termites in the trunk of the family tree.
> *a conscience*—The tragedy of the second lie is that it is always easier to tell than the first.
> *a career*—Just ask the student who got booted out for cheating or the employee who got fired for embezzlement if the lie wasn't fatal. . . .

We could also list the deaths of intimacy, trust, peace, credibility, and self-respect. But perhaps the most tragic death that occurs from deceit is our [Christian] witness. The court won't listen to the testimony of a perjured witness. Neither will the world.

Just Like Jesus

Read Together

No one who is dishonest will live in my house;
no liars will stay around me.

PSALM 101:7

142

The Cost of Lies

More than once I've heard people talk about the story of Ananias and Sapphira (Acts 5:1–11) with a nervous chuckle and say, "I'm glad God doesn't still strike people dead for lying." But I'm not so sure that he doesn't. It seems to me that the punishment for lying is still death. Not death of the body, maybe, but death of: *a parent's trust*—Lies are like termites in the trunk of the family tree; *a conscience*—The real sadness of the second lie is that it's always easier to tell than the first; *a future*—Just ask the student who was flunked for cheating if that lie was really worth it.

We could also list the deaths of friendships, trust, peace, reputation, and self-respect. But perhaps the most tragic death that happens because of our lies is the death of our Christian witness. Courtrooms and judges won't listen to witnesses who lie. And neither will the world.

GROWING IN GRACE

Why do you think people lie? Ananias and Sapphira lied to make themselves look good. Others may lie to get out of trouble or to get something they want. The problem with one lie is that it usually leads to another and another. Lies are kind of like onions—lots of layers and all of them stink!

Who Can Fathom Eternity?

It doesn't take a wise person to know that people long for more than earth. When we see pain, we yearn. When we see hunger, we question why. Senseless deaths. Endless tears, needless loss. . . .

We have our moments. The newborn on our breast, the bride on our arm, the sunshine on our back. But even those moments are simply slivers of light breaking through heaven's window. God flirts with us. He tantalizes us. He romances us. Those moments are appetizers for the dish that is to come.

"No one has ever imagined what God has prepared for those who love him" (1 Corinthians 2:9).

What a breathtaking verse! Do you see what it says? *Heaven is beyond our imagination. . . .* At our most creative moment, at our deepest thought, at our highest level, we still cannot fathom eternity.

When God Whispers Your Name

Read Together

God has planted eternity in the hearts of men.

ECCLESIASTES 3:11 TLB

Beyond Our Imagination

It doesn't take a genius to know that we want more than this earth can give us. We wish for a place free of pain and hunger. Free of sickness and tears and loss. And sometimes we find ourselves asking, "Why is life so hard?"

So God gives us moments of joy. The loving hug of a parent, the comfort of a true friend, the warm sunshine on our back. These are his gifts of hope to us—like tiny slivers of light breaking through the window of heaven. God gives us these glimpses of joy to give us hope and keep us going. He is saying to us, "If you think this is good, just wait and see what I have for you in heaven."

As Paul quoted, "No one has ever imagined what God has prepared for those who love him" (1 Corinthians 2:9 ICB).

What an amazing verse! Do you see what it says? Heaven is *beyond* our imagination. Even in our most creative moments, in our wildest dreams, we cannot imagine the wonder and perfection of heaven.

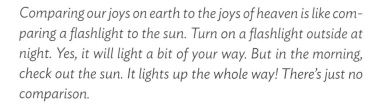

GROWING IN GRACE

Comparing our joys on earth to the joys of heaven is like comparing a flashlight to the sun. Turn on a flashlight outside at night. Yes, it will light a bit of your way. But in the morning, check out the sun. It lights up the whole way! There's just no comparison.

Sweeter After a Rest

Time has skyrocketed in value. The value of any commodity depends on its scarcity. And time that once was abundant now is going to the highest bidder. . . .

When I was ten years old, my mother enrolled me in piano lessons. . . . Spending thirty minutes every afternoon tethered to a piano bench was a torture. . . .

Some of the music, though, I learned to enjoy. I hammered the staccatos. I belabored the crescendos. . . . But there was one instruction in the music I could never obey to my teacher's satisfaction. The *rest*. The zigzagged command to do nothing. What sense does that make? Why sit at the piano and pause when you can pound?

"Because," my teacher patiently explained, "music is always sweeter after a rest."

It didn't make sense to me at age ten. But now, a few decades later, the words ring with wisdom—divine wisdom.

The Applause of Heaven

Read Together

In six days the LORD made everything. . . . On the seventh day he rested.

EXODUS 20:11

Sweeter After a Rest

When I was ten years old, my mother made me take piano lessons. Spending thirty minutes every afternoon on that piano bench was torture.

Some of the music, though, I learned to enjoy. I hammered the staccatos. I pounded the crescendos. But there was one instruction in the music I could never get quite right. The *rest*. That zigzag-looking sign to do nothing. What sense does that make? Why sit at the piano and pause when you can pound?

"Because," my teacher patiently explained, "music is always sweeter after a rest."

It didn't make sense to me then. But now my teacher's words ring with wisdom—divine wisdom. Music is sweeter after a rest. And life is sweeter after you rest in the Lord.

GROWING IN GRACE

Your life can get pretty crazy. There are family things and church things, school things and sports things. Things can take over, so take time to rest in God. Just spend some time hanging out in his presence. You'll find that the world is much sweeter after you rest from it.

God's Name in Your Heart

When you are confused about the future, go to your *Jehovah-raah,* your caring shepherd. When you are anxious about provision, talk to *Jehovah-jireh,* the Lord who provides. Are your challenges too great? Seek the help of *Jehovah-shalom,* the Lord is peace. Is your body sick? Are your emotions weak? *Jehovah-rophe,* the Lord who heals you, will see you now. Do you feel like a soldier stranded behind enemy lines? Take refuge in *Jehovah-nissi,* the Lord my banner.

Meditating on the names of God reminds you of the character of God. Take these names and bury them in your heart.

God is

the shepherd who guides,
the Lord who provides,
the voice who brings peace in the storm,
the physician who heals the sick, and
the banner that guides the soldier.

The Great House of God

Read Together

The name of the LORD is a strong tower;
    the righteous run to it and are safe.

PROVERBS 18:10 NKJV

The Names of God

God has many names to show how he meets your many needs.

When you are confused about the future, go to your *Jehovah-raah*, your caring shepherd. When you are worried about the things you need, talk to *Jehovah-jireh*, the Lord who provides. Do your troubles seem too large? Seek the help of *Jehovah-shalom*, the Lord is peace. Is your body sick? Is your heart hurting? *Jehovah-rophe*, the Lord who heals you, will see you now. Do you feel like a soldier stuck behind enemy lines? Keep your eyes on *Jehovah-nissi*, the Lord is the flag that I follow.

Thinking about the names of God reminds you of the character of God. Take these names and hide them in your heart.

God is . . . the *shepherd* who guides, the *Lord* who provides, the *voice* who brings peace in the storm, the *physician* who heals the sick, and the *flag* that the soldier follows.

GROWING IN GRACE

What are your names? Not just your first, middle, and last names, but your other names—like son or daughter, brother or sister, friend, student. Just as each of your names tells something different about who you are and what you do, so God's names tell all the different things he does for you.

Focus on God's Majesty

Some years ago a sociologist accompanied a group of mountain climbers on an expedition. Among other things, he observed a distinct correlation between cloud cover and contentment. When there was no cloud cover and the peak was in view, the climbers were energetic and cooperative. When the gray clouds eclipsed the view of the mountaintop, though, the climbers were sullen and selfish.

The same thing happens to us. As long as our eyes are on God's majesty there is a bounce in our step. But let our eyes focus on the dirt beneath us and we will grumble about every rock and crevice we have to cross. For this reason Paul urged, "Don't shuffle along, eyes to the ground, absorbed with the things right in front of you. Look up, and be alert to the things going on around Christ—that's where the action is. See things from his perspective" (Colossians 3:1–2 MSG).

The Great House of God

Read Together

You have not seen Christ, but still you love him. You cannot see him now, but you believe in him.

1 PETER 1:8

Keep Your Eyes on God

Some years ago a sociologist—a person who studies how people act—went with a group of mountain climbers on an expedition. One of the things he noticed was the connection between clouds and contentment. Where there were no clouds and the climbers could see the peak of the mountain, they were full of energy and eager to help one another. But when dark, gray clouds blocked their view of the mountaintop, the climbers became bad-tempered and selfish.

The same thing happens to us. As long as our eyes are on God's majesty, there is a bounce in our step. We are happy with ourselves and happy to help others. But let our eyes focus on the dirt of this world, and we will grumble about every rock and mud puddle we have to step over. Because of this, Paul urged us to "think only about the things in heaven, not the things on earth" (Colossians 3:2 ICB).

GROWING IN GRACE

Keep a weather journal for a week. Write down if the weather is warm or cold, sunny or cloudy. Also write down how you feel on those days. Does sunshine give you energy? Do clouds make you blue? If dark days drag you down, focus on the Son when there's no sun in the sky.

In the Arms of God

We don't like to say good-bye to those whom we love. Whether it be at a school or a cemetery, separation is tough. It is right for us to weep, but there is no need for us to despair. They had pain here. They have no pain there. They struggled here. They have no struggles there. You and I might wonder why God took them home. But they don't. They understand. They are, at this very moment, at peace in the presence of God. . . .

When it is cold on earth, we can take comfort in knowing that our loved ones are in the warm arms of God. And when Christ comes, we will hold them, too.

When Christ Comes

Read Together

"Everyone who lives and believes in me will never die."

JOHN 11:26

In the Arms of God

We don't like to say good-bye to the people we love. Whether it is saying good-bye to a friend who moves away or to a loved one who has passed away, being apart from the ones we love is hard. When death is the reason for our good-bye, it is especially tough. It is right for us to be sad and to cry, but we don't have to give up hope. Remember: They had pain here on earth, but they have no pain there in heaven. They struggled here on earth, but they have no struggles there in heaven.

You and I might wonder why God took them to heaven. But they don't. They understand. They are, at this very second, at peace and with God.

When it is cold here on earth, we can take comfort in knowing that our loved ones are safe in the warm arms of God. And when Jesus comes back, we will see them again.

GROWING IN GRACE

Ask your parents if your family can plant a tree to honor a lost loved one. Pick a spot where you will be able to see it often. As you watch it grow, know that the God who created this tree from a tiny seed is watching over your loved one—just as you are watching over your tree.

The Doorway to Your Heart

Your heart is a fertile greenhouse ready to produce good fruit. Your mind is the doorway to your heart—the strategic place where you determine which seeds are sown and which seeds are discarded. The Holy Spirit is ready to help you manage and filter the thoughts that try to enter. He can help you guard your heart.

He stands with you on the threshold. A thought approaches, a questionable thought. Do you throw open the door and let it enter? Of course not. You "fight to capture every thought until it acknowledges the authority of Christ" (2 Corinthians 10:5 PHILLIPS). You don't leave the door unguarded. You stand equipped with handcuffs and leg irons, ready to capture any thought not fit to enter.

Just Like Jesus

Read Together

If people's thinking is controlled by the sinful self, there is death. But if their thinking is controlled by the Spirit, there is life and peace.

ROMANS 8:6

Guarding Your Heart

Your heart is like a greenhouse ready to grow good fruit. And your mind is the doorway to that greenhouse, to your heart. It is in your mind that you decide which seeds are planted in your heart and which seeds are thrown away. Which thoughts are worth hanging on to and which ones need to be weeded out. The Holy Spirit is ready to help you sort out all those thoughts that try to get in. He can help you guard your heart.

The Holy Spirit stands with you in the doorway. If a thought approaches, a thought that may not be so good, do you throw open the door and let it enter? Of course not. You "capture every thought and make it give up and obey Christ" (2 Corinthians 10:5 ICB). You don't leave the door wide open and unguarded. You stand ready with handcuffs and leg irons, ready to capture any thought not good enough to enter.

GROWING IN GRACE

Some thoughts are clearly good. Others are clearly bad. And some are kind of in between. How can you tell which are good and which are bad? Ask yourself, Would I want others to know I'm thinking this thought? Would I want Jesus to know? If not, then toss it out!

Waiting Forwardly

Great question. What kind of people should we be? Peter tells us: "You should live holy lives and serve God, as you wait for and look forward to the coming of the day of God" (2 Peter 3:11–12).

Hope of the future is not a license for irresponsibility in the present. Let us wait forwardly, but let us wait.

But for most of us, waiting is not our problem. Or, maybe I should state, waiting *is* our problem. We are so good at waiting that we don't wait *forwardly*. We forget to look. . . . We are too content. We seldom search the skies. . . . We seldom, if ever, allow the Holy Spirit to interrupt our plans and lead us to worship so that we might see Jesus.

When Christ Comes

Read Together

The day of the Lord will come like a thief. The skies will disappear with a loud noise. . . . So what kind of people should you be?

2 PETER 3:10–11

156

Expecting Jesus

What kind of people should we be? Great question. Peter told us, "You should live holy lives and serve God. You should wait for the day of God and look forward to its coming" (2 Peter 3:11–12 ICB).

The hope of heaven in the future, though, does not give us the right to do whatever we want today. We should be holy and wait for the Lord.

We wait on a lot things. We wait in line, in class, in the car—and we wait *expecting* our wait to end. But how are we waiting for Jesus? Are we expecting our wait for him to end? Are we looking for him? Too often we are content to just wait, and we forget to *expect*. We don't let the Holy Spirit change our plans. We don't let him lead us to worship so that we might see Jesus. We are waiting, but we are not expecting.

GROWING IN GRACE

What does "waiting for Jesus" mean? It's a lot like waiting for a vacation. You're counting down the days, but you're also busy getting ready. Packing. Making lists. Deciding which way to go. You're waiting, but you're waiting busily. Wait for Jesus busily too. Pray. Study. Teach. Get ready.

A Faithful Father

To recognize God as Lord is to acknowledge that he is sovereign and supreme in the universe. To accept him as Savior is to accept his gift of salvation offered on the cross. To regard him as Father is to go a step further. Ideally, a father is the one in your life who provides and protects. This is exactly what God has done.

He has provided for your needs (Matthew 6:25–34).

He has protected you from harm (Psalm 139:5).

He has adopted you (Ephesians 1:5). And he has given you his name (1 John 3:1).

God has proven himself as a faithful father. Now it falls to us to be trusting children.

He Still Moves Stones

Read Together

He is a faithful God who does no wrong, who is right and fair.

DEUTERONOMY 32:4

A Faithful Father

To know God as Lord is to know that he is Ruler and King of all the universe. To accept him as Savior is to accept his gift of salvation that he offered through Jesus on the cross. To see him as Father is to go a step further. A father should be the one in your life who provides for you and protects you. Earthly fathers sometimes fail at this, but God does not. See what he has done for you:

He has taken care of all your needs (Matthew 6:25–34).
He has protected you from harm (Psalm 139:5).
He has adopted you as his own child (Ephesians 1:5).
And he has given you his name (1 John 3:1).

God has proven himself to be a faithful Father. Now it is up to us to be trusting children.

GROWING IN GRACE

Just as your parents have responsibilities toward you, you have responsibilities to your parents. To obey. Respect. Love. Listen. You have those same responsibilities to God. After all, he is your Father.

A Treasure Map

The Bible has been banned, burned, scoffed, and ridiculed. Scholars have mocked it as foolish. Kings have branded it as illegal. A thousand times over it the grave has been dug, and the dirge has begun, but somehow the Bible never stays in the grave. Not only has it survived, it has thrived. It is the single most popular book in all of history. It has been the best-selling book in the world for years!

There is no way on earth to explain it. Which perhaps is the only explanation. The answer? The Bible's durability is not found on earth; it is found in heaven. For the millions who have tested its claims and claimed its promises there is but one answer—the Bible is God's book and God's voice. . . .

The purpose of the Bible is to proclaim God's plan and passion to save his children. That is the reason this book has endured through the centuries. . . . It is the treasure map that leads us to God's highest treasure, eternal life.

The Inspirational Study Bible

Read Together

In the beginning there was the Word. The Word was with God, and the Word was God.

JOHN 1:1

160

A Treasure Map

The Bible has been banned, burned, made fun of, and laughed at. Scholars have called it foolish. Kings have made it illegal. A thousand times over the Bible has been declared dead, but somehow it never stays in the grave. Not only has it survived all these years, but it has also thrived. It is the single most popular book in all of history—the best-selling book in the world for years!

There is no way on earth to explain it, which is perhaps the only way to explain it. The answer for the Bible's survival is not found on earth; it is found in heaven. The Bible is God's book and God's voice. It cannot be silenced.

The purpose of the Bible is to tell the world of God's plan and his passion to save his children. That is the reason the Bible has survived for centuries. It is the treasure map that leads us to God's greatest treasure—eternal life with him in heaven.

GROWING IN GRACE

Hide a treasure—a candy bar or a couple of cookies. Make a treasure map with clues showing how to find it. Give it to a friend and see if he or she can find the treasure. As wonderful as it is to find your treasure, how much more wonderful will it be to find God's treasure for you?

Confident in the Father

If you'll celebrate a marriage anniversary alone this year, God speaks to you.

If your child made it to heaven before making it to kindergarten, he speaks to you. . . .

If your dreams were buried as they lowered the casket, God speaks to you.

He speaks to all of us who have stood or will stand in the soft dirt near an open grave. And to us he gives this confident word: "I want you to know what happens to a Christian when he dies so that when it happens, you will not be full of sorrow, as those are who have no hope. For since we believe that Jesus died and then came back to life again, we can also believe that when Jesus returns, God will bring back with him all the Christians who have died" (1 Thessalonians 4:13–14 TLB).

When Christ Comes

Read Together

The LORD comforts his people
and will have pity on those who suffer.

ISAIAH 49:13

162

God Speaks to You

At one time or another, we all have to deal with the death of some-one we love. God understands your hurt, and he wants to comfort you.

If you'll celebrate a birthday without a beloved grandparent by your side, God speaks to you. If a parent went to heaven far too soon, God speaks to you. If you're still missing a friend who passed away, God speaks to you.

God speaks to all who have stood or will stand in the soft dirt near an open grave. And he gives us these words of comfort: "I want you to know what happens to a Christian when he dies so that when it happens, you will not be full of sorrow, as those are who have no hope. For since we believe that Jesus died and then came back to life again, we can also believe that when Jesus returns, God will bring back with him all the Christians who have died" (1 Thessalonians 4:13–14 TLB).

GROWING IN GRACE

If someone you love has passed away, write down the things you loved about that person. Add a photo or a drawing. When you are missing that person, take out your list and take time to remember. Ask God to hold your loved one close until you are together again.

In a Word

Think for a moment about this question: What if God weren't here on earth? You think people can be cruel now, imagine us without the presence of God. You think we are brutal to each other now, imagine the world without the Holy Spirit. You think there is loneliness and despair and guilt now, imagine life without the touch of Jesus. No forgiveness. No hope. No acts of kindness. No words of love. No more food given in his name. No more songs sung to his praise. No more deeds done in his honor. If God took away his angels, his grace, his promise of eternity, and his servants, what would the world be like?

In a word, hell.

Just Like Jesus

Read Together

He who overcomes, and keeps My works until the end, to him I will give power over the nations.

REVELATION 2:26 NKJV

In a Word

Think for a minute about this question: What if the Spirit of God weren't here on earth? If you think people can be mean now, imagine what we would be like without the presence of God! If you think we are hateful to each other now, imagine the world without the Holy Spirit. If you think there is loneliness and sadness and guilt now, imagine life without the touch of Jesus.

No forgiveness. No hope. No acts of kindness. No words of love. No more food given in his name. No more songs sung to his praise. No more good deeds done in his honor. If God took away his angels, his grace, his promise of eternal life, and his servants, what would the world be like?

In a word: empty. I'd much rather have a world full of Jesus.

GROWING IN GRACE

Imagine a world without the sun. What would happen? Darkness. Cold. Plants and animals would die. People would starve. Now think of what would happen without God. Spiritual darkness. Cold hearts. Dying souls. People starving for love. Just as the sun gives us physical light and life, God gives us spiritual light and life.

No Secrets from God

Have you been there? Have you felt the ground of conviction give way beneath your feet? The ledge crumbles, your eyes widen, and down you go. *Poof!*

Now what do you do? . . . When we fall, we can dismiss it. We can deny it. We can distort it. Or we can deal with it. . . .

We keep no secrets from God. Confession is not telling God what we did. He already knows. Confession is simply agreeing with God that our acts were wrong. . . .

How can God heal what we deny? . . . How can God grant us pardon when we won't admit our guilt? Ahh, there's that word: *guilt*. Isn't that what we avoid? Guilt. Isn't that what we detest? But is guilt so bad? What does guilt imply if not that we know right from wrong, that we aspire to be better than we are. . . . That's what guilt is: a healthy regret for telling God one thing and doing another.

A Gentle Thunder

Read Together

If anyone belongs to Christ, there is a new creation. The old things have gone; everything is made new!

2 CORINTHIANS 5:17

166

No Secrets from God

Have you been there? You knew what was right. You knew what was wrong. And you chose wrong. It's like you were standing on the edge of the cliff, trying to make a decision, and the ground of your goodness just crumbled under your feet. The ledge gave way, and down you went. *Poof!*

Now what do you do? When you fall, you can forget it. You can fib about it. Or you can face it.

We can keep no secrets from God. Confession is not telling God what we did. He already knows. Confession is simply agreeing with God that what we did was wrong.

How can God forgive if we don't admit our guilt? Ahh, there's that word: *guilt*. Isn't that what we want to avoid? What we hate? But is guilt so bad? Guilt simply means that we know right from wrong, that we hope to do better next time. Guilt is a healthy sorrow for telling God one thing but then doing another.

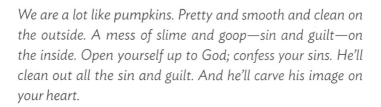

GROWING IN GRACE

We are a lot like pumpkins. Pretty and smooth and clean on the outside. A mess of slime and goop—sin and guilt—on the inside. Open yourself up to God; confess your sins. He'll clean out all the sin and guilt. And he'll carve his image on your heart.

A Plate of Experiences

Last night during family devotions, I called my daughters to the table and set a plate in front of each. In the center of the table I placed a collection of food: some fruit, some raw vegetables, and some Oreo cookies. "Every day," I explained, "God prepares for us a plate of experiences. What kind of plate do you most enjoy?"

The answer was easy. Sara put three cookies on her plate. Some days are like that, aren't they? Some days are "three-cookie days." Many are not. Sometimes our plate has nothing but vegetables— twenty-four hours of celery, carrots, and squash. Apparently God knows we need some strength, and though the portion may be hard to swallow, isn't it for our own good? Most days, however, have a bit of it all. . . .

The next time your plate has more broccoli than apple pie, remember who prepared the meal. And the next time your plate has a portion you find hard to swallow, talk to God about it. Jesus did.

The Great House of God

Read Together

"I have good plans for you, not plans to hurt you."

JEREMIAH 29:11

A Plate of Cookies

One night during family devotions, I set an empty plate in front of each of my daughters. In the center of the table, I placed a collection of fruit, raw vegetables, and Oreo cookies. "Every day," I explained, "God prepares for us a plate of experiences. What kind of plate do you most enjoy?"

The answer was easy. Sarah put three cookies on her plate. Some days are like that, aren't they? Some days are "three-cookie days." But many are not. Sometimes our plate has nothing but vegetables—twenty-four hours of celery, carrots, and squash. God knows we need to build up our muscles. It may be hard to swallow, but isn't it for our own good? Most days, however, have a little bit of everything.

The next time your plate—er, day—has more "broccoli" than "Oreos," remember who made it. And if you're finding it all a little hard to swallow, talk to God about it. Jesus did.

GROWING IN GRACE

Most days have a little bit of everything in them. A little good, a little bad. A little mad, sad, and glad. Get yourself ready for those days with a plateful of God's food—a little prayer, a little study, a little praise—and you'll be ready to face the world.

Run the Race

The word *race* is from the Greek *agon,* from which we get the word *agony.* The Christian's race is not a jog but rather a demanding and grueling, sometimes agonizing race. It takes a massive effort to finish strong.

Likely you've noticed that many don't? Surely you've observed there are many on the side of the trail? They used to be running. There was a time when they kept the pace. But then weariness set in. They didn't think the run would be this tough. . . .

By contrast, Jesus' best work was his final work, and his strongest step was his last step. Our Master is the classic example of one who endured. . . . He could have quit the race. But he didn't.

Just Like Jesus

Read Together

Let us run the race that is before us and never give up.

Hebrews 12:1

Finishing the Race

The word *race* comes from the Greek word *agon,* from which we get the word *agony.* The writer of Hebrews compares the Christian's life to a race. This race is not an easy jog, but rather a demanding, hard, sometimes *agonizing* race. It takes a huge effort to finish strong.

Unfortunately, many Christians don't finish the race. Maybe you've seen some who are stopped on the side of the trail of life. They used to be running, living their lives for Christ. There was a time when they kept up. But then they became tired. They never thought the race would be this tough.

Think about Jesus and the race he ran. Jesus' best work was his final work, and his strongest step was his last step to the cross. Our Lord is the best example of One who kept going. He could have quit. But he didn't. He finished the race. By his grace, you will too.

GROWING IN GRACE

Have you ever run in a race? It's pretty easy when you start. But then it gets harder. How do you feel halfway through? Tempted to quit? But catch one glimpse of that finish line, and you're filled with energy. How great it is to finish!

Got It All Figured Out

We understand how storms are created. We map solar systems and transplant hearts. We measure the depths of the oceans and send signals to distant planets. We . . . have studied the system and are learning how it works.

And, for some, the loss of mystery has led to the loss of majesty. The more we know, the less we believe. Strange, don't you think? Knowledge of the workings shouldn't negate wonder. Knowledge should stir wonder. Who has more reason to worship than the astronomer who has seen the stars? . . .

Ironically, the more we know, the less we worship. We are more impressed with our discovery of the light switch than with the one who invented electricity. . . . Rather than worship the Creator, we worship the creation (see Romans 1:25).

No wonder there is no wonder. We've figured it all out.

In the Grip of Grace

Read Together

I look at your heavens,
     which you made with your fingers. . . .

PSALM 8:3

All Figured Out

Scientists understand how storms are created. They can map out the solar systems, measure the depths of the oceans, and send signals to faraway planets. They have studied our world, and they are learning how it works.

And, for some people, this loss of mystery has led to the loss of majesty. The more they know about the world, the less they believe in God. That's strange, don't you think? Knowing how things work shouldn't erase the wonder. It should stir up the wonder.

Yet the more some people know about our world, the less they worship God. They are more impressed with our invention of the lightbulb than with the One who created electricity. Rather than worship the Creator, they worship the creation (Romans 1:25). No wonder there is no wonder. They think they've got it all figured out.

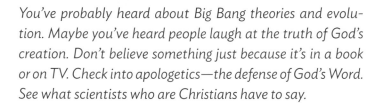

GROWING IN GRACE

You've probably heard about Big Bang theories and evolution. Maybe you've heard people laugh at the truth of God's creation. Don't believe something just because it's in a book or on TV. Check into apologetics—the defense of God's Word. See what scientists who are Christians have to say.

A Compassionate God

My child's feelings are hurt. I tell her she's special.

My child is injured. I do whatever it takes to make her feel better.

My child is afraid. I won't go to sleep until she is secure.

I'm not a hero. . . . I'm a parent. When a child hurts, a parent does what comes naturally. He helps. . . .

Why don't I let my Father do for me what I am more than willing to do for my own children?

I'm learning. . . . Being a father is teaching me that when I am criticized, injured, or afraid, there is a Father who is ready to comfort me. There is a Father who will hold me until I'm better, help me until I can live with the hurt, and who won't go to sleep when I'm afraid of waking up and seeing the dark.

Ever.

The Applause of Heaven

Read Together

He comforts us every time we have trouble, so when others have trouble, we can comfort them.

2 CORINTHIANS 1:4

174

God Is Ready to Help

A parent's job is to help his children when they are hurt. Think about your own parents and all that they do for you: When your feelings are hurt, do they tell you how amazing you really are? When you've been hurt, do they do whatever it takes to make you feel better? When you are afraid, do they wait with you until you feel safe?

That's what parents are supposed to do. They help their hurting children. But what if you are away from your parents, maybe at school? Or if your parents aren't the helping kind?

Then remember you have a heavenly Father who is always ready to help. When you are laughed at, hurt, or afraid, he is ready to comfort you. He will hold you until you're better, help you until you can live with the hurt, and stay with you when you're afraid of waking up and seeing the dark.

Always.

GROWING IN GRACE

How many good things have your parents done for you just today? Be sure to give them a huge thank-you. But as much as your parents love you, God loves you a million-billion times more. You can't begin to imagine how many good things he will do for you . . . just today.

Saying "Thank You"

Worship is when you're aware that what you've been given is far greater than what you can give. Worship is the awareness that were it not for his touch, you'd still be hobbling and hurting, bitter and broken. Worship is the half-glazed expression on the parched face of a desert pilgrim as he discovers that the oasis is not a mirage.

Worship is the "thank you" that refuses to be silenced.

We have tried to make a science out of worship. We can't do that. We can't do that any more than we can "sell love" or "negotiate peace."

Worship is a voluntary act of gratitude offered by the saved to the Savior, by the healed to the Healer, and by the delivered to the Deliverer.

In the Eye of the Storm

Read Together

Thank the LORD because he is good.
His love continues forever.

PSALM 106:1

Saying "Thank You"

Worship is what happens when you are aware that the gift you've been given is far greater than anything you can give.

Worship is like the traveler who is lost in the desert. The one thing he wants more than anything is the one thing he can't seem to find—water. So when he does finally find that pool of water, he just can't help but shout out his thankfulness.

Worship is the thank you that just can't be quiet.

Sometimes people try to make a science out of worship, with rules for our songs and for our prayers. But worship isn't supposed to be about rules—it's supposed to be so much more.

Worship is the heart's thank you . . . offered by the one who is saved to the Savior, by the one who is healed to the Healer, and by the one who is delivered to the Deliverer.

GROWING IN GRACE

There are many ways to worship God. Try a different way today. Paint a picture of praise. Sing a song of salvation. Write a poem of his promises. Say thank you in a whole new way.

A Place for the Weary

Is there anything more frail than a bruised reed? Look at the bruised reed at the water's edge. A once slender and tall stalk of sturdy river grass, it is now bowed and bent.

Are you a bruised reed? Was it so long ago that you stood so tall, so proud? . . .

Then something happened. You were bruised . . .

by harsh words
by a friend's anger
by a spouse's betrayal. . . .

The bruised reed. . . . Society knows what to do with you. . . . The world will break you off; the world will snuff you out.

But the artists of Scripture proclaim that God won't. Painted on canvas after canvas is the tender touch of a Creator who has a special place for the bruised and weary of the world. A God who is the friend of the wounded heart.

He Still Moves Stones

Read Together

Do not lose the courage you had in the past, which has a great reward.

HEBREWS 10:35

178

A Place for the Tired

The reed. It's a slender and tall stalk of river grass. Yet it's so fragile, so easily bruised. What once stood so proud and strong can easily be knocked over at the edge of the water.

Sometimes we can be like bruised reeds. Maybe we stood so tall and so proud once, thinking life was just right. Then something happened. We were bruised by mean words, someone's anger, or a friend's betrayal.

The bruised reed. This world knows what to do with us when we're no longer standing up tall. This world wants to break us so that we can never stand up tall again.

But the Bible tells us that God won't do that. He has a special place for people who are bruised and tired. And God will help us stand up tall again.

GROWING IN GRACE

Imagine the way a mother bird shelters her babies. She tucks them up under her wing, warm and safe from all harm. That is just what God wants to do for you when you are hurting. "He will protect you like a bird spreading its wings over its young" (Psalm 91:4 ICB).

Spiritual Life from the Spirit

Perhaps your childhood memories bring more hurt than inspiration. The voices of your past cursed you, belittled you, ignored you. At the time, you thought such treatment was typical. Now you see it isn't.

And now you find yourself trying to explain your past. Do you rise above the past and make a difference? Or do you remain controlled by the past and make excuses?

Think about this. Spiritual life comes from the Spirit! Your parents may have given you genes, but God gives you grace. Your parents may be responsible for your body, but God has taken charge of your soul. You may get your looks from your mother, but you get eternity from your Father, your heavenly Father. And God is willing to give you what your family didn't.

When God Whispers Your Name

Read Together

Now we do not live following our sinful selves, but we live following the Spirit.

ROMANS 8:4

Dare to Be Different

Some people are not who they should be. Instead of giving friendship and encouragement to those around them, they treat them unkindly. They laugh at others and make fun of them. Sometimes they pretend that others just aren't important enough for them to even notice. We call them bullies. God calls them lost.

So what do you do? What do you do when the bullies are the popular kids everyone else wants to be like? Do you dare to be different? Do you dare to be the person God made you to be? Or do you just go along with the crowd and be like them?

It's your choice, but you don't have to make it alone. Jesus himself said, "You can be sure that I will be with you always" (Matthew 28:20 ICB). *Always.* When the bullies laugh, when the in-crowd puts you in the out-crowd, Jesus will be there with you.

GROWING IN GRACE

If you or someone you know is being picked on or bullied, what can you do? First, pray and ask God to bring people into your life to help you. Then talk to a trusted grown-up—a parent, someone from church, or a teacher. God uses his people to answer your prayers.

Run to Jesus

Do you wonder where you can go for encouragement and motivation? Go back to that moment when you first saw the love of Jesus Christ. Remember the day when you were separated from Christ? You knew only guilt and confusion and then—a light. Someone opened a door and light came into your darkness, and you said in your heart, "I am redeemed!"

Run to Jesus. Jesus wants you to go to him. He wants to become the most important person in your life, the greatest love you'll ever know. He wants you to love him so much that there's no room in your heart and in your life for sin. Invite him to take up residence in your heart.

Walking with the Savior

Read Together

If we live, we are living for the Lord, and if we die, we are dying for the Lord.

ROMANS 14:8

Turn to Jesus

Do you ever feel like you're all alone? Like no one else could possibly understand how you're feeling? Do you wish there was someone you could turn to for encouragement, for hope, for courage? There is. Jesus.

Turn to Jesus and his love. When you feel like your friends have all left you. When you know you've messed up and you're not sure how to make it right. Turn to Jesus. Ask him to take away your confusion and guilt. Ask him to show you the right thing to do. And trust him to always love you and help you through the hard times.

Jesus wants you to turn to him. He wants to be the most important person in your life, the greatest love you'll ever know. He wants you to love him so much that there's no room in your heart and in your life for sin. Ask him to come and live in your heart. He won't say no.

GROWING IN GRACE

Zacchaeus climbed a tree to see Jesus. Four friends ripped open a roof to see Jesus. What will you do to see Jesus? Will you choose church over a ball game? Bible class over a movie? Prayer time over play time? Choose Jesus, and I promise you'll be glad you did.

A True Family

Does Jesus have anything to say about dealing with difficult relatives? Is there an example of Jesus bringing peace to a painful family? Yes there is.

His own. . . .

It may surprise you to know that Jesus had a family at all! You may not be aware that Jesus had brothers and sisters. He did. Quoting Jesus' hometown critics, Mark wrote, "[Jesus] is just the carpenter, the son of Mary and the brother of James, Joseph, Judas, and Simon. And his sisters are here with us" (Mark 6:3).

And it may surprise you to know that his family was less than perfect. They were. If your family doesn't appreciate you, take heart, neither did Jesus'. . . .

Yet he didn't try to control his family's behavior, nor did he let their behavior control his. He didn't demand that they agree with him. He didn't sulk when they insulted him. He didn't make it his mission to try to please them.

He Still Moves Stones

Read Together

"My true brother and sister and mother are those who do what God wants."

MARK 3:35

Jesus' Family

It may surprise you to know that Jesus had brothers and sisters. But he did. Mark wrote this about Jesus' family: "His mother is Mary. He is the brother of James, Joseph, Judas, and Simon. And his sisters are here with us" (Mark 6:3 ICB).

And it may also surprise you to know that Jesus' family was less than perfect. They were human, after all. Mark even told us that Jesus' family didn't always understand him and why he was preaching. Once, they even tried to stop his preaching and take him home because "people were saying that Jesus was out of his mind" (Mark 3:21 ICB).

How do you think Jesus treated his family when they didn't agree with him or understand him? The same way he treated all people. With kindness and patience, with love and respect. And that's just how he wants you to treat your family—even when they don't understand you and you don't understand them.

GROWING IN GRACE

What does God say about dealing with difficult people? Check out these verses: Don't hold a grudge (Proverbs 10:12). Just let it go (19:11). But most of all, love them anyway and pray for them (Matthew 5:44).

185

God Is for You

God is *for* you. Turn to the sidelines; that's God cheering your run. Look past the finish line; that's God applauding your steps. Listen for him in the bleachers, shouting your name. Too tired to continue? He'll carry you. Too discouraged to fight? He's picking you up. God is for you.

God is for *you*. Had he a calendar, your birthday would be circled. If he drove a car, your name would be on his bumper. If there's a tree in heaven, he's carved your name in the bark. . . .

"Can a mother forget the baby at her breast and have no compassion on the child she has borne?" God asks in Isaiah 49:15 (NIV). What a bizarre question. Can you mothers imagine feeding your infant and then later asking, "What was that baby's name?" No. I've seen you care for your young. You stroke the hair, you touch the face, you sing the name over and over. Can a mother forget? No way. But "even if she could forget, . . . I will not forget you," God pledges (Isaiah 49:15).

In the Grip of Grace

Read Together

He will rejoice over you.
　　You will rest in his love;
　　he will sing and be joyful about you.

ZEPHANIAH 3:17

God Is for You

Let's pretend that life is like a big race. Look at the sidelines—that's God cheering you on. Look past the finish line—that's God clapping. Listen for him in the bleachers, shouting your name. Too tired to finish? He'll carry you. Too hopeless to keep going? He'll pick you up. God is *for* you.

God is for *you*. If he had a calendar, your birthday would be circled. If he drove a car, your name would be on his bumper sticker. If there's a tree in heaven, he's carved your name in it.

"Can a woman forget the baby she nurses? Can she feel no kindness for the child she gave birth to?" God asks in Isaiah 49:15 (ICB). Can you imagine your mom feeding you and then asking, "What is that kid's name?" No. Mothers don't do that. They stroke your hair, touch your face, sing your name over and over. Do mothers forget? No way. But "even if she could forget . . . I will not forget you," God promises (Isaiah 49:15 ICB).

GROWING IN GRACE

Do something today to show your mom how much you love her. Thank her for all she does for you. Offer to help with the dishes. Take out the trash. Write her a note. If she asks why, tell her it's just because you love the way she loves you.

The Cure for Disappointment

When God doesn't do what we want, it's not easy. Never has been. Never will be. But faith is the conviction that God knows more than we do about this life, and he will get us through it.

Remember, disappointment is cured by revamped expectations.

I like the story about the fellow who went to the pet store in search of a singing parakeet. Seems he was a bachelor and his house was too quiet. The store owner had just the bird for him, so the man bought it.

The next day the bachelor came home from work to a house full of music. He went to the cage to feed the bird and noticed for the first time that the parakeet had only one leg.

He felt cheated that he'd been sold a one-legged bird, so he called and complained.

"What do you want," the store owner responded, "a bird who can sing or a bird who can dance?"

Good question for times of disappointment.

He Still Moves Stones

Read Together

The ways of God are without fault.

PSALM 18:30

188

What Do You Expect?

I like the story about the fellow who went to the pet store to buy a singing parakeet. The man lived alone, and his house was too quiet. The store owner said he had just the bird for him, so the man bought it.

The next day the man came home from work to a house full of music. He went to feed the bird and saw for the first time that it had only one leg. He felt cheated that he'd been sold a one-legged bird, so he called the store and complained.

"What do you want," the store owner asked, "a bird that can sing or a bird that can dance?"

Good question. God always answers our prayers. But sometimes it's not the answer we expect—like the man's one-legged bird. And we're disappointed. When that happens, we have to ask ourselves: *What do we really want?* Remember, God only wants the very best for you. So if his answer is not what you expect, maybe you need to *change* what you expect.

GROWING IN GRACE

Disappointments can be as bitter as lemons. Ask a grown-up to help you make homemade lemonade. Sample the lemon first. Sour, hmmm? Then taste the lemonade. Much better! When you add the sweetness of God (sugar) to your disappointments (lemons), they can turn out to be blessings (lemonade).

Prayer Reminds Us

Prayer is the recognition that if God had not engaged himself in our problems, we would still be lost in the blackness. It is by his mercy that we have been lifted up. Prayer is that whole process that reminds us of who God is and who we are.

I believe there's great power in prayer. I believe God heals the wounded, and that he can raise the dead. But I don't believe we tell God what to do and when to do it.

God knows that we, with our limited vision, don't even know that for which we should pray. When we entrust our requests to him, we trust him to honor our prayers with holy judgment.

Walking with the Savior

Read Together

When a believing person prays, great things happen.

JAMES 5:16

Let God Decide

When we pray, we are telling God that we need him. We are admitting that without him, we know we would never make it to heaven. It is only by his mercy that we are lifted up and saved. Prayer reminds us of *who God is* (the One in charge) and *who we are* (the one he loves enough to help).

I believe there's great power in prayer. I believe that God heals the sick and wounded and that he can raise the dead. But I don't believe we tell God what to do and when to do it.

God knows that sometimes we don't even know what we should pray for. When we trust our prayers to him, we trust him to do what is right for us—even if it's not what we asked for. We let God decide what is best.

GROWING IN GRACE

Sometimes we don't know how to explain what we're feeling. It's okay. God has a plan for that: "The Spirit himself speaks to God for us, even begs God for us. The Spirit speaks to God with deep feelings that words cannot explain" (Romans 8:26 ICB). Just open your heart to God, and let the Holy Spirit speak.

Grace Upon Grace

Test this question: What if God's only gift to you were his grace to save you? Would you be content? You beg him to save the life of your child. You plead with him to keep your business afloat. You implore him to remove the cancer from your body. What if his answer is, "My grace is enough"? Would you be content?

You see, from heaven's perspective, grace is enough. If God did nothing more than save us from hell, could anyone complain? . . . Having been given eternal life, dare we grumble at an aching body? Having been given heavenly riches, dare we bemoan earthly poverty? . . .

If you have eyes to read these words, hands to hold this book, the means to own this volume, he has already given you grace upon grace.

In the Grip of Grace

Read Together

I have learned to be satisfied with the things I have and with everything that happens.

PHILIPPIANS 4:11

Can We Really Complain?

Ask yourself this question: What if the only gift God ever gave you was his grace—his forgiveness so that you can be saved and go to heaven? Would you be happy?

Maybe you've begged God to help you pass a test. Or find your lost pet. Or even heal someone you love. What if his answer is, "No. My grace is enough. Saving you is enough"? Would you be happy?

You see, from heaven's point of view, grace *is* enough. If the only thing God did was save us, could we really complain? If he only gave us eternal life, would we dare grumble about a hurting body? If he only gave us all the riches of heaven, would we dare whine about being poor on earth?

If you have eyes to read these words and hands to hold this book, God has already given you a mountain of grace. But because he loves you so much, he doesn't just give you grace. He answers your prayers too.

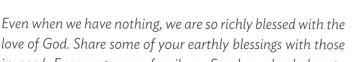

GROWING IN GRACE

Even when we have nothing, we are so richly blessed with the love of God. Share some of your earthly blessings with those in need. Encourage your family or Sunday school class to adopt a family who's struggling. Bring in gifts and groceries. Secretly deliver them with a note that says, "A gift from God."

God Isn't Hard to Find

What a surprising way to describe God. A God who pursues us.

Dare we envision a mobile, active God who chases us, tracks us, following us with goodness and mercy all the days of our lives? He's not hard to find. He's there in Scripture, looking for Adam and Eve. They're hiding in the bushes, partly to cover their bodies, partly to cover their sin. Does God wait for them to come to him? No, the words ring in the garden. "Where are you?" God asks (Genesis 3:9), beginning his quest to redeem the heart of man. A quest to follow his children until his children follow him.

The Gift for All People

Read Together

Surely goodness and mercy shall follow me
    all the days of my life.
and I will dwell in the house of the LORD forever.

PSALM 23:6 NKJV

God Isn't Hard to Find

As a child, it's fun to play hide-and-seek. But that is a game that God never plays. You see, God never hides; he always seeks.

God started seeking his children right there in Genesis. He was there in the garden, looking for Adam and Eve. They were hiding in the bushes, ashamed and afraid. Did God wait for them to come to him? No, his words rang out through the garden. "Where are you?" God asked (Genesis 3:9).

Now, God knew where Adam and Eve were hidden, but he wanted them to know that he was searching for them. That he hadn't left them all alone. And he wanted them to come out and find him. All through the Bible God calls out to his children, hoping that they will come out and find him.

He's calling to you too. He's not hard to find. He's only a word away. Pray that he will help you find him today.

GROWING IN GRACE

Where are you? Are you hard for God to find? Are you hoping he won't see what you're doing? Are you hoping he won't hear what you're laughing about with your friends? If you are hoping that God doesn't know what you're up to, maybe you need to change what you're up to.

Because of Our Need

Can you imagine prospective parents saying, "We'd like to adopt Johnny, but first we want to know a few things. Does he have a house to live in? Does he have money for tuition? Does he have a ride to school every morning and clothes to wear every day? Can he prepare his own meals and mend his own clothes?"

No agency would stand for such talk. Its representative would lift her hand and say, "Wait a minute. You don't understand. You don't adopt Johnny because of what he has; you adopt him because of what he needs. He needs a home."

The same is true with God. He doesn't adopt us because of what we have. He doesn't give us his name because of our wit or wallet or good attitude. . . . Adoption is something we receive, not something we earn.

The Great House of God

Read Together

"For God did not send His Son into the world to condemn the world, but that the world through Him might be saved."

JOHN 3:17 NKJV

Because of What You Need

Can you imagine parents who want to adopt a child saying, "We'd like to adopt Johnny, but first we want to know a few things. Does he have a house to live in? Does he have money for college? Does he have a ride to school every morning and clothes to wear every day? Can he cook his own meals and wash his own clothes?"

No adoption agency would listen to such talk. The agent would hold up her hand and say, "Wait a minute. You don't understand. You don't adopt Johnny because of what he has. You adopt him because of what he needs. He needs a home."

The same is true with God. He doesn't give you his name because of your great sense of humor or your talents or your money. He doesn't adopt you because of what you have. He adopts you because of what you need—him.

GROWING IN GRACE

Ask three people—one your age, one your parents' age, one your grandparents' age—about the greatest gifts they've ever been given. How are their gifts different? The same? Does it make you look at the gifts you've been given differently? Or the gifts you want to give?

The Strength of God's Love

"Can anything make me stop loving you?" God asks. "Watch me speak your language, sleep on your earth, and feel your hurts. Behold the maker of sight and sound as he sneezes, coughs, and blows his nose. You wonder if I understand how you feel? Look into the dancing eyes of the kid in Nazareth; that's God walking to school. Ponder the toddler at Mary's table; that's God spilling his milk.

"You wonder how long my love will last? Find your answer on a splintered cross, on a craggy hill. That's me you see up there, your maker, your God, nail-stabbed and bleeding. Covered in spit and sin-soaked.

"That's your sin I'm feeling. That's your death I'm dying. That's your resurrection I'm living. That's how much I love you."

In the Grip of Grace

Read Together

God shows his great love for us in this way: Christ died for us while we were still sinners.

ROMANS 5:8

The Strength of God's Love

When you read about Jesus' life on earth, it's as if he is saying, "Can anything make me stop loving you? Watch me speak your language, sleep on your earth, and feel your hurts. Look at me! The Maker of all that you see. Watch me sneeze, and cough, and blow my nose. You wonder if I understand how you feel? See the toddler at Mary's table; that's God spilling his milk. Look into the dancing eyes of that kid playing with his friends in Nazareth; that's God walking to school.

"Do you want to know how much I love you? I love you enough to leave heaven. To be a toddler and stub my toe as I learn to walk. To smash my thumb in the carpenter's shop. I love you enough to be insulted by the very people I created. To be betrayed by my friends. To die on the cross for you. That's how much I love you."

GROWING IN GRACE

What are the strongest things you can think of? Steel? Concrete? Superman? Dynamite? They are nothing compared to the strength of God—nothing! "I am sure that nothing can separate us from the love God has for us" (Romans 8:38 ICB).

God Changes Families

God has proven himself as a faithful father. Now it falls to us to be trusting children. Let God give you what your family doesn't. Let him fill the void others have left. Rely upon him for your affirmation and encouragement. Look at Paul's words: "you are God's child, and *God will give you the blessing he promised*, because you are his child" (Galatians 4:7, emphasis added).

Having your family's approval is desirable but not necessary for happiness and not always possible. Jesus did not let the difficult dynamic of his family overshadow his call from God. And because he didn't, [his family] chapter has a happy ending. . . .

He gave them space, time, and grace. And because he did, they changed. . . . One brother became an apostle (Galatians 1:19) and others became missionaries (1 Corinthians 9:5).

He Still Moves Stones

Read Together

They all continued praying together with some women, including Mary the mother of Jesus, and Jesus' brothers.

ACTS 1:14

200

God Is Faithful

Friends are the people we go to for encouragement and a listening ear. But sometimes even our friends can hurt us. Maybe a friend has said something hurtful. Maybe a friend has betrayed you. Or maybe a friend has recently moved away.

A troubled friendship can leave you feeling empty and hurt inside. Jesus understands. After all, Judas was his friend, and Judas betrayed him. Peter was his friend, and Peter said he didn't even know him. John was his friend, and he ran away when Jesus was arrested.

Friends aren't always faithful, but God is. So the next time a troubled friendship leaves you hurt, ask God to comfort you. Ask him to fill that emptiness with his peace. And then pray for your friend—God can touch the heart of your friend too.

GROWING IN GRACE

Some people are hard to get along with. Although you can't change what others do, make sure you aren't part of the problem. "Show mercy to others; be kind, humble, gentle, and patient. Do not be angry with each other, but forgive each other. If someone does wrong to you, then forgive him" (Colossians 3:12–13 ICB).

A PRAYER FOR WHEN YOU WISH YOU WERE BRAVE

Teach kids how to manage their fears and worries and learn to trust God with this hilarious new picture book.

Follow a silly series of misadventures as scaredy-cat faces his worst fears. For each of the fears, Max provides this reassuring child's version of Philippians 4:6–9:

"God, you are good. God, you are near. God, you are here! And, God, you love me."

Available wherever books are sold.

GOD ANSWERS THE CHALLENGES
OF LIFE WITH ONE WORD: GRACE

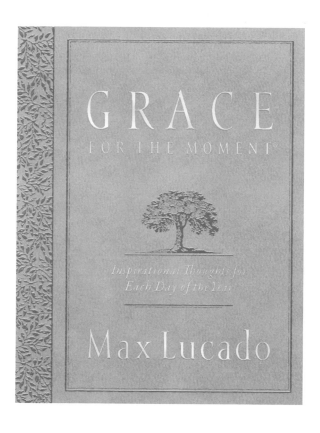

In this easy-to-read, comfort-size print 365-day devotional,
Max Lucado reminds us that ups and downs may
mark our days, but God fills our lives with grace.

Give Your Child the Gift
of God's Grace Every Day

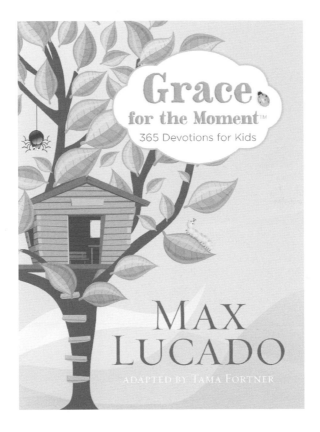

Adapted from the bestselling devotional for
adults, Max Lucado presents the message of God's
grace in a way that children can understand.